IPSWICH TOWN
UNCOVERED

IPSWICH TOWN
UNCOVERED

Dave Allard   **Neal Manning**

First published in Great Britain in 2012 by The Derby Books Publishing Company Limited, 3 The Parker Centre, Derby, DE21 4SZ.

ISBN 978-1-78091-201-1

Printed and bound by Gomer Press, Llandysul, Ceredigion.

Contents

Acknowledgements

Our sincerest and heartfelt thanks:

- To Martin White for his thorough editing and reading of the book. He would be disappointed if there was even a comma out of place – and if there is, it's not his fault!
- To Owen Hines and David Kindred for supplying nearly all of the photographs from bygone days. (In all other cases every effort has been made to trace the photographer(s).)
- To those who have supplied many of the stories – most notably Ted Phillips, Ken Hancock and Bob Shelley. It's been great catching up!
- To Debbie Charman, who co-ordinated, filed and administered the authors' stories. If it had been left to Dave and Neal, God knows what would have happened!
- To Paul Driver and the staff at the Kesgrave Kitchen for their hospitality. It was within your walls that the idea for the book was hatched in the first place.
- To Steve, Dianne and Simon and all at DB Publishing for their help and support.
- And to Stephen Allard for his help with the structure of the book and his help with publication.

Dave Allard and Neal Manning
October 2012

Foreword
Back in the Day

Sports journalists Dave Allard and Neal Manning are Suffolk football reporting legends. Between them they have covered Ipswich Town for 50 years, starting with the Jackie Milburn era in 1963, when it was just Neal, right through to the present day, which sees Dave soldiering gladly on in his freelance capacity for *The Daily Mirror*. In many ways it has been a roller-coaster ride, highs and lows all over, as the boys have followed by far the greatest side in Anglia through their various trials and tribulations, but as you're about to see, they never lost their sense of humour or love for the club. In their time, both working for the Ipswich-based *East Anglian Daily Times*, *Evening Star* and the Saturday night football paper, the *Green 'Un*, they have travelled from Arsenal to Aberdeen, Rotherham to Rome and Torquay to Twente Enschede to cover the fortunes of the Suffolk club.

Now they bring you **Ipswich Town Uncovered**. A football book with a difference, it takes you behind the glory and the cameras and, with only a few holds barred to protect the slightly less than innocent, they reveal the best of their stories from the last 50 years, many of which have never been told before.

It would be impossible to produce a book like this of the modern game. Technology has meant that little is secret, while the relationship between managers, players and journalists is nothing like it used to be. We now live in an age dominated by electronic gadgets, computers and mobile phones. Press conferences are regimented, permission is sought to speak to players and even questions sometimes have to be seen in advance by the club's Press office! Today, clubs go to great lengths to keep journalists at arms' length and in many cases only tolerate them because they have to. In addition, editors put pressure on writers to reveal every spit and cough and to leave no stone unturned. It's little wonder that relationships are most often strained. It's all a far cry from Dave and Neal's experience back in the day, when players and journalists regularly socialised – having a game of golf or going out for a meal and a beer or three. A lot of what was said remained 'in-house'. Players and managers used to tell journalists stories that were 'off the record', meaning they must not be published. Breaking this trust meant any relationship would come to an abrupt end, and this was a code clearly understood by all concerned. But that said, don't imagine for one moment, that nothing controversial was ever reported. A lot of it was, but the relationship between managers, players and journalists was such that some incidents never saw the light of day on the front or back pages.

Until Now! Yes, now two of our greatest authorities on the post Sir Alf era reveal a treasure chest of stories which never made the papers and, purely for legal reasons, some of them – shame I hear you cry! – have to be told without naming names. Everything herein though, the boys swear most solemnly on Sir Alf's and Sir Bobby's statues, is absolutely true. From the late, great 'Wor' Jackie Milburn right through to Roy Keane and featuring in particular the 13-year reign of the late, great Sir Bobby Robson, this book offers a fascinating insight into the personalities of the various managers at Portman Road over the past 50 years. Packed full of stories and surprises the boys have loved every minute of reliving their professional lives and times and are sure you're going to love reading about an Ipswich Town you haven't read too much about before

So hold on tight to the rollercoaster ladies and gentlemen. And enjoy.

JACKIE MILBURN

January 1963–September 1964   Neal Manning

JACKIE MILBURN was a legend as a player. A swashbuckling centre-forward for Newcastle and England, he was idolised on Tyneside, his native home, especially by Newcastle United supporters, who first christened him 'Wor Jackie'. Every week he had St James's Park packed to the rafters as he banged in the goals and rightly gained legendary status, but sadly it was just the opposite when he tried his hand at management.

Skittled!

Jackie was appointed manager of Ipswich Town in January 1963 following Alf Ramsey's departure to take the England job, but the very likeable Geordie was not suited for the cut-throat world he was about to enter.

'He was a smashing bloke, but he wasn't a manager,' recalled Ted Phillips whose goalscoring exploits helped Town win the Third Division South, Second and First Division titles. Recalling one of Jackie's stranger managerial strategies Ted goes on, 'Jackie decided that twice a week we would go ten-pin bowling instead of training on the practice pitch. All the players moaned, but Jackie insisted that we went to the bowling alley and the winner on each given day was paid a monetary prize by him.' Jackie never explained why ten-pin bowling should be beneficial to a group of players that were fighting for their First Division survival, and even though they survived relegation at the end of the 1962-63 season, the writing was on the wall and the following campaign (Jackie's only full one in charge), they went down, finishing rock bottom and having been skittled for an embarrassing total of 121 goals, which can't have helped the already fragile party atmosphere down at the local bowling alley. A 10-1 humiliation at Fulham on Boxing Day and a 9-1 hammering at Stoke were just two of the lowest points of that season, but an incident at Blackpool probably summed up best why Jackie was simply not up to the job.

The night before the Saturday match, chairman John Cobbold and another director, along with trainer Jimmy Forsyth and Jackie were having a late drink in the hotel. All of a sudden two members of the playing staff strolled in and straight past them at 2am. Jackie did not stop them to ask where they had been and never said a word about it either then or later. Imagine that today! As it was, Town gained a point in a 2-2 draw at Bloomfield Road, so presumably he thought all was well and least said soonest mended.

But all was obviously not well. As things plunged from bad to worse, Jackie simply did not know how to arrest the slide. He turned to Tony Garnett for advice, who covered Town matches for the *East Anglian Daily Times* in those days, as the supporters were definitely becoming restless. And there was many a time on a Friday night before a home match when Jackie and Tony came into the EADT Press Club for a late-night drink. A card school was in full flow on one side of the room and other journalists and printers were all enjoying a drink while the pair of them set about the serious task of picking the Town side to play the following day!

Back to Ted Phillips who recalls perhaps one of the key final nails in 'Wor Jackie's' Portman Road coffin. 'I couldn't understand why he sold Ray,' he say, remembering how shocked he was when Ray Crawford, his old striking partner, was sold to Wolverhampton Wanderers a month after the start of the 1963-64 season. 'But then he asked me to play centre-forward. That's not my position, I told him. I'm not playing up front. The following week he pulled me into his office and said that Leyton Orient were interested in signing me. I couldn't wait to get on the train to London and I scored a hat-trick in my first game for them.'

Soon afterwards, Jackie had gone as well.

JACKIE MILBURN

January 1963–September 1964   Dave Allard

Booze, boos and bread rolls

ALTHOUGH 'Wor' Jackie's spell in charge at Ipswich Town has to go down as a bit of a disaster, it must never be forgotten that his abiding legacy to the club was that he started the youth policy. By the time he left at the end of his 18 month reign, the youngsters were enjoying playing in the Mercia League and junior talent began to abound at Portman Road. Regularly attracting gates of 5,000 plus at Portman Road on Tuesday nights, players like Mick Mills, Colin Viljoen were in the side at the time and they both went on to become full England internationals. Town then entered the South Eastern Counties League, arguably the top youth competition in the country and where some household names at the time had started their careers, so in the sense of planting the seed from which so many of our future stars were to grow, he forever left a little bit of 'Wor Jackie' here in Suffolk.

Town chairman John Cobbold, who was known to one and all as 'Mr John', once told me: 'He was Wor Jackie up there and we wanted him to become Wor Jackie here, but sadly he decided he'd had enough and resigned.' He went on, 'I really wanted him to stay and pleaded with him to give it a bit longer, but his wife Laura said that perhaps the job was starting to affect his health, so I accepted Jackie's decision.'

At Ipswich, John Cobbold thought the world of Jackie, and the feeling was mutual, although the manager was constantly amazed at the zany antics by the chairman of the Blues' board. Jackie said: 'We were in a hotel once having an evening meal. Suddenly, the sweet trolley was wheeled in by a waiter. Mr John was sitting on it and he was carrying a load of bread rolls. He began throwing them at us. I was startled and thought we would possibly be asked to leave the hotel.' He added: 'I mentioned my fears about that to Mr John, but he said: 'Don't worry old boy, the chairman of this hotel chain is my old chum from schooldays at Eton'.'

To be fair to Jackie's period of tenure it has to be said that following Alf Ramsey on such limited managerial experience- merely a short stint previously as player/manager of Linfield in Ireland – was a hard act to follow, but Jackie stacked the club with far too many below average players and, as Neal has already said, club discipline wasn't as strict as it should have been, as he trusted people a bit too much. One of his most successful signings was Joe Broadfoot from Millwall, a favourite of the fans who was to become a real key figure. He told me, 'I thought the world of Jackie, but he was such a worrier. I was usually bubbling before a match. If I was a bit quiet Jackie would fuss around me and start fretting. Jackie was too nice to be a manager. He was a national treasure, but not a football manager.'

While Mr John wanted Jackie to continue, other directors knew that something had to give as the club were floundering near the bottom of the old Second Division following relegation from the top flight.

One director told me: 'Jackie trusted players too much. He was a dedicated professional himself and didn't believe that some of his players were not looking after themselves as they should.' He went on, 'A big drinking culture developed at the club. The club was out of control and Jackie was too nice a guy to put it right. He saw the good in everyone, not the darker side. The club needed better players and better discipline.'

Ipswich players were seen drinking most nights of the week in some of the roughest pubs in town and sometimes on a Friday night before a home match. The whip had to be cracked and sadly, 'Wor Jackie' was not the man to do it. The man who had scored 200 goals for his beloved Magpies went back to the north-east and worked as a football reporter for a Sunday newspaper.

I once spent a long time talking to him at St James's Park before an Ipswich game and in his soft, broad Geordie accent, he declared: 'Hey, bonny lad – Ipswich. What a super club and what a super place. They treated me so well, but it was not for me.'

How appropriate it was then that Town should be the visitors when the Jackie Milburn Stand was opened by Laura in 1988. Jackie had died of lung cancer not long before aged 64. He won three FA Cup winners medals with Newcastle, and, besides a stand, has two statues in his honour. One is in his home town of Ashington and the other is close to Newcastle's ground. A fitting tribute to a footballing legend, whose greatness as a player was never ever in doubt.

BILL McGARRY

October 1964–November 1968   Neal Manning

New broom – stand by your beds!

BILL McGARRY certainly made his mark during his reign at Portman Road. Appointed in the wake of Jackie Milburn's departure, the former England wing-half took Town from the bottom of the old Second Division to champions in 1968 before he suddenly resigned just three months into their First Division campaign.

When Bill arrived at Portman Road in October 1964, he came with a reputation as a hard man who would certainly not suffer fools gladly. And, sure enough, he soon made his presence felt, even though he upset some of the more established players. Reputations would count for nothing as far as Bill was concerned as he went about the job of lifting Town up the Second Division table. Town finished fifth at the end of that first season, losing only four of the 31 League matches he was in charge of.

Town continued to make progress, reaching the fifth round of the FA Cup, where they were drawn against First Division side Manchester City at Maine Road. City were one of the best teams in the country at the time with the likes of Mike Summerbee, Colin Bell and Francis Lee in their side, so everyone was well aware of the size of the challenge.

Bill decided to take the players to Southport for five days leading up to the tie. I went with them and it proved to be quite an eventful time. Training – and I had to join in – was on the beach; then it was game of squash, at which

Bill was particularly good; followed by a round of golf at Royal Birkdale. The only thing that Bill didn't know about and orchestrate in the midst of all this was a trip out to a local nightclub.

And just as well. One player got so drunk he finished up lying in the gutter. He was picked up by the police at 5am and returned to the hotel with Bill completely oblivious as to what had gone on. Had McGarry found out, that player would have been sent straight home. As it was he had an outstanding match as Town shocked their high-flying opponents by earning a 1-1 draw.

There was, however, to be no fairytale ending as City won 3-0 in the replay at Portman Road. Summerbee, who missed the first game with hamstring trouble, scored twice although he reckoned he was only 10 per cent fit.

The following season Town were crowned Second Division champions after going on a 15 match unbeaten run to finish off the campaign. Indeed, it was at Carlisle in mid-February where Town suffered only one of five defeats in the League all season.

Bill was not on the team coach that headed north on the Friday afternoon to make their overnight stop at Darlington. He was away completing the signings of Peter Morris and John O'Rourke, leaving coach Sammy Chung in charge.

Sammy was a nice guy and the players knew it. Straight after dinner we all headed to a pub and stayed there until closing time. Whether this had an effect on the 4-1 defeat we shall never know, but one thing's for sure, a trip out to a Darlington boozer wouldn't have been on the agenda had Bill been there. The players told Sammy they were going to the pictures and he was totally unaware they had something very different in mind! Which reminds me of another incident in Plymouth that passed under the Bill radar, where a certain Town player took a swing at a somebody in a group of sailors on shore leave, but missed and instead connected with the jaw of Bill Baxter, who was minding his own business and talking to somebody else. We got kicked out for that, but managed to get our heads down in the midnight sleeper home with Bill, Sammy and the directors who'd stayed back at the hotel while we went out none the wiser. So despite the new strict regime, a good time was still occasionally had by all, as Bill's bandwagon rolled on and ended with promotion back to the big time.

Bigger ponds, smaller fish

But three months into that new campaign the bandwagon came juddering to a halt, when Bill asked to be released from his contract, which he had signed only a few months earlier, to take over as manager of Wolverhampton Wanderers from Ronnie Allen.

On the day the news was released, I went round to see him at his house in Henley Road, Ipswich. Bill and I had got on well during his stay at the club, both on a working and social level – despite having the odd spat. To be honest I couldn't understand why he had suddenly decided to leave a club that he had taken into the top flight of English football. I implored him to change his mind. 'Don't go Bill,' I remember saying. 'You could be making the biggest mistake of your life.'

He didn't disagree, but quickly added: 'Wolves is a much bigger club than Ipswich and I can't turn down the chance to manage them. If I said no to Wolves now I might never get the opportunity to manage a big club again.'

I pointed out to him that he had a job for life at Ipswich if he wanted it and if he continued to have the success he had already achieved. However, the overriding factor for Bill was that to have the chance to manage a club like Wolverhampton Wanderers was too good an opportunity to turn down.

'It will bring you problems Bill,' I said. 'The expectancy level will be far greater than it is at Ipswich.' He agreed, but it was the challenge that excited him at a club with a great tradition and history.

I was sorry to see Bill go, and so was my sports editor, Alan Everett, who played a lot of golf with him at Woodbridge. Whenever Bill played golf with someone he had never met, he always said: 'My name's McGarry and I don't look for golf balls.'

Perhaps the irony of Bill's departure and Bobby Robson taking over was that at the end of that season, Town finished six points ahead of Wolves to end in a mid-table position.

After leaving Wolves, Bill was appointed manager of the Saudi Arabia national team and after a spell abroad he took over at Newcastle United. Not long after joining them, I received a call from John Gibson, then sports editor of *The Evening Chronicle*. Newcastle were hovering around mid-table and not making the progress for which their demanding supporters hoped.

As far as the *Chronicle* was concerned, they simply couldn't get on with Bill and the man who was covering the club decided he'd had enough. So Gibson rang me, more out of desperation than anything else, to ask if I fancied his job. 'You get on with him well. Bill seems the sort of person who is OK if you know him. What he doesn't appear to understand is the passion of the supporters and their desire to know everything. And he doesn't take kindly to criticism.'

I was flattered by John's offer, but the move up north was a non-starter for me as I had divorced a couple of years earlier, and with a couple of very young children, moving 300 miles away would have meant seeing very little of them.

As it was, Bill only lasted one season at St James's Park.

In the days before we had to kick racism out of football

Yes, that's how long ago we're talking ladies and gentlemen. Back in Bill's day we were still light years away from a properly multi-cultural talent pool and one day I remember getting a phone call from Bill a month into the first season back in the First Division. I was sitting in the office one afternoon when he rang to seek my opinion on whether or not he should sign Steve Stacey from Wrexham.

The reason was that Stacey was black and Bill was concerned about the reaction of some supporters. After making a steady start to the campaign, Town had been hit by injuries to Tommy Carroll and Bill Baxter and the manager needed to sign a replacement.

I simply said: 'If he can play, it won't matter what colour he is, or whether he's an Eskimo or a Red Indian.' Bill seemed reassured and on the Saturday Stacey made his debut at home to Liverpool. However, after half-an-hour he was carried off with a thigh injury in a 2-0 defeat and only played two more first team games before being sold to Bristol City a year later.

Reg pulls a fast one on Spurs

Reg Tyrrell was a larger-than-life character who had joined the Portman Road staff as chief scout. Bill had brought him from Bournemouth and he doubled up his scouting duties by being in charge of the youth set-up that had been started by Jackie Milburn.

It had been a masterstroke by Jackie and Town played in the Mercia Youth League, regularly attracting gates of 5,000-plus at Portman Road on Tuesday nights.

Town were very successful in the South East Counties League, but on one occasion Reg, who seldom missed a trick, was struggling for players for a SECL match against Tottenham at Cheshunt one Saturday morning in the late 1960s.

He often came round to the sports room at the *East Anglian Daily Times*, but on a particular Friday morning his reason for popping in was to see David Sandilands who worked for the *Suffolk Press*, then part of our company's empire.

Reg seemed to know all about 'Sandy', who had very youthful – almost schoolboy – looks despite now being 19. 'Spurs won't know we're playing an over-age player,' he said as I took him to meet 'Sandy'.

Now in his early 60s, 'Sandy' recalls that game. 'When we arrived at the ground, goalkeeper Laurie Sivell cut his head against the boot of the team bus and had to play with a bandage around the injury. I remember Trevor Whymark also played for us, while Graeme Souness was playing for Spurs and he ran the game which they won 1-0.'

Hanks a lot Bill!

Ken Hancock was one of McGarry's first signings in December 1964, and the former Port Vale goalkeeper proved an inspirational capture.

'He was a funny man,' he recalls. 'I admired his abilities, but found him difficult to like.'

He told me about a time when he was at loggerheads with McGarry and had been left out of the side for a couple of games with David Best back in the side.

He said: 'I had been playing squash one afternoon when someone told me that the boss wanted to see me. David Best had dislocated a bone in his leg, and Bill said to me, "What would you do if I told you that you were playing against Manchester United at Old Trafford on Saturday?"' To which Hank responded, 'You're wondering if I will chuck a couple of goals in just to spite you. Well, contrary what you might be thinking, I will play out of my skin.' And with that Hank got up and walked out of his office.

Come Saturday Ken was as good as his word and played what he modestly described as 'a blinder' to help Town earn a point in a goalless draw. But there was to be no praise from McGarry, and the 'keeper said, 'The biggest compliment he ever paid me was "you had a good game today Hank, but I think your brother Ray [who also played for Port Vale] is a better goalkeeper than you!"'

Yet for all that 'Hank' regarded McGarry as a good manager, if a bit unfathomable. He recalled the occasion when the boss made him play against Arsenal with the aid of an injection. 'Frank Wignall had stamped on me during a First Division game against Wolves on the first day of the season. I had to carry on as there were no substitute goalkeepers in those days. I missed the next three matches, but then he talked me into playing against Arsenal at home. So I had an injection in my right leg – my kicking leg – but when I took my first goal-kick, I collapsed in incredible pain. I said to Billy Houghton that he would have to take the goal-kicks. At half-time Bill said to me "you're not fit" and I said, "I've been telling you that for a week!" So I had another injection, and Bobby Hunt almost passed out!'

In total 'Hank' made 180 appearances for Town including being ever present in the Second Division winning side of 1968. He said: 'I analysed everything about goalkeeping, and I have never come across a manager who has understood the art of goalkeeping, including Bill Nicholson in my time at Tottenham. And there was no better manager than Bill.'

Ken, like so many footballers, was superstitious. For every match he prepared in exactly the same way, even to the point that he always drove exactly the same way to Portman Road. 'The only person I gave a lift to was Danny Hegan. If I saw somebody else I knew standing on the pavement, I would drive past. The only trouble was that Danny was always late. One day we were due to go play at Birmingham City, and the boss told us that we had to be at the station by 9am. We were only a few minutes late, but that wasn't good enough for Bill. He fined us £20 each for being late. "When I say 9am I mean 9am!" he said.

'Anyway we both had cracking games, and on the train back from the Midlands we were having a meal, when the boss came up to us and said that we could forget the fines. That was Bill McGarry all over.'

No photo finish – take that Bill!

Colin Macer, a photographer on the *East Anglian and Daily Times* in the 1960s, did not have any time for Bill McGarry. Colin found him rude and unhelpful when he went to Portman Road. But a few years later he exacted his revenge when the two of them met by chance. Colin had left Suffolk and was working as a resident photographer at Heathrow airport.

Bill was manager of Wolverhampton Wanderers at the time and he and his team were at the airport preparing to fly out for a pre-season tour. Bill spotted Colin as the team were waiting to board their plane and asked him if he would take a picture. Colin agreed and went to work to set up the photograph, asking the players and McGarry and his staff to stand on the steps leading into the plane.

Then the snapper decided it was pay back time. Instead of taking a picture, he held two fingers up to McGarry before turning his back and walking away!

BILL McGARRY

October 1964–November 1968   Dave Allard

Plastered and angry

TOWN directors knew full well that the whip needed cracking after the more – ahem! – relaxed regime that prevailed during the short reign Jackie Milburn. Bill McGarry, as you've heard, was the tough guy appointed, and never mind cracking the whip, at one stage during his Town career he cracked a bone in his lower leg.

Bill got so angry after a bad home display that he kicked a big dressing room door stop in anger. On the Monday morning, the ex-Bournemouth and Watford chief turned up with a heavy plaster cast on the affected leg. No one dare laugh. Most people at the club were in fear of him and I saw it at first hand for a time when I was an associate schoolboy at the club.

You might call it old school...

I used to turn up on Thursday nights for training with a group of aspirants that included Brian Talbot, who was later to play for England as an Ipswich player before moving to Arsenal.

First team coach Sammy Chung would sometimes take the training, but usually it was Ray Coe, with chief scout Reg Tyrrell hovering around. One night Reg and Ray came into the dressing room and declared in unison: 'Look lively boys, look lively boys. McGarry is coming, McGarry is coming.' Both of them were almost rigid with fear.

In he came and just before we went out for a full-scale practice match, Bill said: 'Go out there and play as if your life depends on it. And play hard. We don't carry passengers here. You're all here for a reason, but if you're not up to it you'll be out.'

Then he turned to Talbot, a teammate of mine in the Suffolk county schoolboy squad, and roared: 'Where have you been lately, Mr bloody Talbot. You can't just drift in here when you want. If you want to go to a bigger club, then go to a bigger club. If not, then we want you here every week.'

My pal Keith Broxton said to me as we went out: 'Blimey, the first team players must shake with fear every day.' Bill was hard and spoke his mind.

The former Huddersfield and England right-half even put chairman John Cobbold firmly in his place soon after joining the club.

Mr John introduced the new boss to his squad in the dressing room. Bill then took the floor and, before speaking to the players, declared: 'Mr Chairman. This is the first and last time you will be in my dressing room.' Not the best foot to get off on you might think, but Bill knew he was on safe ground.

When Town finished their 1968 old Second Division championship title-winning season with a 1-1 home draw against Blackburn in front of a 27,000 crowd, Mr John allowed Bill on the microphone. He probably wished he hadn't.

I recall listening to a sombre-sounding Bill say: 'Perhaps you supporters will cheer us on a little bit more next season.'

...with a touch of new school

But while Bill was a hard man, he was widely respected by his players, even though he could be verbally vicious towards those he felt deserved it. Another corker I remember was delivered on a train coming back from an away game he told a defender in front of teammates: 'You've got a yellow streak running right down the middle of your back.'

Ouch! But he was by no means one-dimensional. Like any football boss worth his salt his man-management could sometimes be of the highest order. A story I heard long after he had left Ipswich showed that to the full.

Alan Sunderland was a young player at Wolves under Bill. When he came to play up front for Ipswich at the end of his career, the ex-Arsenal and England man became a good friend of mine. He told me: 'Bill thought a lot of me and I did of him. He once told my dad that he thought I was "poetry in motion". I was elated when dad told me that.'

Derek Dougan, then a seasoned professional, was Bill's target man and also captained Wolves. He was the 'Mr Big' of Molineux in more ways than one.

One day after training, the young Sunderland and Dougan – later to be elected as chairman of the Professional Footballers' Association – became involved in a heated debate. There was a bit of a scuffle and Bill came in to sort it out. He immediately dressed down the teenager for daring to stand up to Dougan, so it was with some surprise when Alan got a call at his digs from Bill's secretary that afternoon.

'I was summoned to the boss's office and went in fearing the worst,' said Alan, but the young starlet was stunned when Bill not only gave him a pay rise but told him he was proud of the way he had stood up to 'The Doog'.

Alan concluded: 'Bill showed really good management skills. He kept Dougan happy – and me.'

Cobbold!

John Cobbold once said that Bill 'sacked' him before the manager left for Wolves in 1968.

Director Ken Brightwell told me: 'We had a board meeting and decided to offer Bill a bumper new deal. Johnny went up to his office to tell him, but came back with tears rolling down his cheeks.'

According to Ken, Mr John declared: 'Gentlemen, Bill has told me to stick this contract up my arse.'

Cobblers!

Yes, Bill could rub plenty of people up the wrong way. Even the cobbler who came to collect the boots to be repaired, is said to have refused to handle Bill's footwear. He was in the club foyer when the no-nonsense manager came out to deposit a pair of boots at his feet with the words: 'Sort those bastards out.'

The cobbler left them on the floor and told the club secretary, Wally Gray, that he would not touch Bill's boots, although Wally managed to persuade him to continue dealing with the players' footwear.

BOBBY ROBSON

January 1969-May 1974   Dave Allard

The Golden Seed

TOWN director Murray Sangster set the ball rolling for Bobby Robson to become the manager at Portman Road. The head of the Thompson and Morgan seed company planted a golden one in the mind of Bobby one rainy night at Portman Road.

Murray was a real character who often used to travel with the team and loved a Friday night trip to a casino. I went with him to one in Sunderland once and he said: 'Follow what I do, Dave, and you won't go far wrong.' Sure enough I did and it was my best gambling experience ever. In the taxi on the way back he told me how his magic touch played a part in the appointment of Bobby.

'I was in the boardroom before a reserve match and Bobby was in the corner nervously sipping a cup of tea,' he recalled. 'I went up and introduced myself and told Bobby that he should apply for the job at our place. He said that he didn't think he stood a chance, having been sacked by Fulham, but I told him to get his application in.'

Bobby duly did and the rest is history.

The incomparable 'Marty'

Soon after settling behind the manager's desk at Ipswich, Bobby said: 'I know that this is a club that will give me a chance. I know that this club will give me time to prove myself,' which was probably partly a veiled reference to the Fulham chairman , none other than the late comedian

Tommy Trinder, who was renowned at the club for his great impatience. But the early days were not comfortable at times for the former England right-half. Senior professionals were of a similar age, or not far short, of the 36-year-old new man and behind his back he was nicknamed 'Marty'. This was because the new boss would often have big bags under his eyes at training in the mornings after returning from a faraway scouting mission the night before and one of the club's apprentice professionals told me at the time: 'The old pros say that the boss's eyes in the morning resemble those of Marty Feldman.' Feldman, who had gaunt features and deep, sunken eyes, was then a top radio and television comic and successful scriptwriter.

Seconds out for the old guard

Not long after Bobby's appointment came a notorious incident involving the manager and first-team players Billy Baxter and Tommy Carroll. Once again, an apprentice professional of the day has given me first-hand, or shall we say a 'first fist' account of what happened.

Senior professionals Baxter, a 1962 First Division Championship winner under Alf Ramsey, and Carroll were left out of the side for a home game with West Bromwich Albion in an FA Cup replay. The pair had also been in the 1968 Second Division championship-winning side under Bill McGarry, but Bobby felt that although both were good players, they were slightly over the hill. His main reason for leaving them out was because he considered them to be a bad influence in the dressing room. The manager did not like either of them and they did not like him. He left them out and also had a notice pinned on the door of the players' lounge which said that players not in the squad should not use the facility.

Town won the game against West Brom 3-0 and afterwards Baxter and Carroll stormed into the dressing room, where an apprentice was sweeping up.

He recalled: 'All hell broke loose. Billy screwed the notice up and rammed it into Robson's face. The boss retaliated and Carroll then began throwing punches. Cyril Lea, a former player and now Town's coach, took Robson's side. Blows were being landed all over the place until a group of younger players restored order.'

Baxter never played for the Town again and soon after left for Hull City. Carroll made the odd appearance before beginning a new chapter of his career at Birmingham.

'Kevin son, you were such a star.'

A new era was dawning for the club and a genuine superstar was steadily growing in stature at Portman Road. Kevin Beattie was the boy, or as Bobby said: 'A boy in the body of a man.'

Not long before he died, Bobby told me: 'I was so, so lucky to get Kevin and he cost us nothing. He turned up at the ground with just a few shillings in his pocket. His clothes were in a battered suitcase that looked like it had been around the world a thousand times, but that boy with loose change in his pocket quickly turned into a pot of solid gold for my club. He became the best English-born player I ever dealt with. He was a diamond.

'Over a long period after getting into the side, he would have been good enough for any team anywhere in the world. His efforts did so much to get us going as a force in the land. He was simply the best.'

Just a few short months before arriving at Ipswich, Liverpool's failure to send someone to pick up triallist Beattie from Lime Street Station meant that the 15-year-old returned to his native Carlisle clubless. Salesman John Carruthers, a part-time Town scout, became a full-time one after retrieving the boy and sending him to Suffolk.

Bobby never believed in having favourites, but he knew he had to build up the starlet Beattie.

Kevin told me: 'The boss used to nip round to my digs to give my landlady, Mrs Vera Strawn, some steaks each week. He wanted me to fill out even more. I was getting extra to what the other apprentices were getting thanks to the boss. I wasn't going to argue after coming from a family of nine in Carlisle where life was tough to say the least.'

How fitting then that the powerful defender now has a letter framed in his Ipswich home that was sent to him in the last year of Bobby's life and a line from it reads: 'Kevin son, you were such a star.'

I left my heart in Millwall, Lincoln and Ipswich

A combination of building a brilliant youth policy, together with shrewd signings, got Bobby and his Town team up among the best in the country. His appointment of ex-Millwall and Lincoln manager Ron Gray as chief scout was also an excellent capture. One of my first meetings with this big, blustery character was just after he had come out of Papworth Hospital following heart surgery.

'Dave my boy,' he said, 'the surgeon said I left one of my heart-strings at Millwall and one at Lincoln.'

Bobby also remembered how Ron announced he was ill. He said: 'Boss, I've got to go into hospital for a few days.'

Bobby asked him why and Ron replied: 'Just a little nick boss, just a little nick.'

That little nick almost took his life and kept him away from Portman Road for three months. After recovering, he continued to serve the club before ending with a testimonial in 1985 when Bobby brought along an England XI to play Ipswich.

BOBBY ROBSON

January 1969–May 1974   Neal Manning

A word in your shell-like

THE phone at my house used to ring every Sunday night without fail. I knew who it was before I answered and for more than an hour on each occasion Bobby wanted to talk about the previous day's game and events at Portman Road in general.

These were the early days of his reign as manager, having been appointed in January 1969. He hadn't been the first choice to succeed Bill McGarry – Bob Stokoe of Carlisle United and Cardiff's Jimmy Scoular were rumoured to have been a couple of the main men in the frame – while one name definitely in it was Billy Bingham, the former Northern Ireland international winger, who was then manager of Plymouth Argyle. An interview for him had been arranged with Town directors, but the day before Bingham informed them that he was staying at Plymouth. That left just Bobby, who impressed chairman John Cobbold and directors Ken Brightwell and Harold Smith at the interview in London. Previous to his ill-fated nine months in charge at Fulham, his only other managerial experience up until this point had been a short spell in Canada as coach of Vancouver Whitecaps.

He did not have an easy ride in his early days at Portman Road, as we've seen from Dave's recollection of that legendary dressing room brawl, and I think that early unease was a big part of the reason for those Sunday night phone calls. He used to pick my brains and even ask advice as he tried to get to grips with the job of keeping Ipswich in the First Division. I'll never forget either those phone calls or his giant will to succeed in his new role that promised so much for the future.

(Shame) There's only one Peter Shilton

The day before Town played Sheffield United at Bramall Lane in March 1974, captain Mick Mills asked me to have a word with Bobby about possibly signing Peter Shilton, then the England goalkeeper.

The Town party were travelling to Sheffield on the Monday afternoon for a Tuesday night First Division game, and as it happened I had arranged with Bobby to do some work with him regarding the Ipswich Town annual that I was writing and editing.

Normally for away trips, there would be directors and the club secretary on the team coach, but being a midweek game, they were travelling up on the day of the match. So, with just Robson, coach Cyril Lea, physiotherapist Brian Simpson and myself occupying the front of the coach, it was an ideal time to speak to Bobby at length without too many interruptions.

Mick had spoken of Shilton's desire to join Town during a previous international get-together with England. Part of the reason was that Ipswich is not that far from Newmarket, the home of racing, and it was well known that England's most capped goalkeeper liked a bet and the chance of moving to a club that was virtually on the doorstep of racing HQ was certainly appealing.

So, at an appropriate moment on that trip north, I broached the subject of Shilton to Bobby. I told him that I understood Shilton would jump at the chance of coming to Portman Road and that the fee would be around the £250,000 mark. That was a lot of money back in 1974, but like Mick Mills, I felt that Shilton could turn Town into a First Division Championship-winning side.

Although initially taken aback that Shilton might be prepared to leave Leicester City, Bobby soon dismissed the idea out of hand. 'I've never paid that sort of money for a player before and I'm not going to start now. Shilton's a good goalkeeper, but I couldn't justify spending that amount of money. It wouldn't be fair to the club.'

Despite trying to persuade him it would be money well spent and that he would almost certainly get a return on his outlay, Bobby wouldn't budge. We hit Sheffield and that was the end of the conservation, but I did mention the subject to him again some years later as the First Division title continued to elude Town.

Bobby's sense of loyalty to the club that had given him his big chance was commendable, as was his fierce loyalty to his players. To the Shilton question he replied, 'It wasn't Paul Cooper's fault that we didn't win the title. Injuries and the number of games we were required to play in a short space of time on several occasions took its toll.'

To be fair, Paul Cooper had proved an excellent signing for a fraction of the money it would have cost to bring Shilton to the club, but it was Nottingham Forest's gain and possibly Town's loss when the England number one joined up with Brian Clough. I know that Bobby's biggest regret in English football was not winning the First Division Championship, although he came close during his 13-year reign at Portman Road, especially in 1981, when Aston

Villa pipped the Blues to the title by just four points. My feeling is that Robson did regret not signing Shilton but was too much of a diplomat to admit it.

Brian Clough had first tried to sign Shilton in 1972 when he was manager of Derby County. Having agreed to pay Stoke City a fee of £175,000, the deal collapsed. When he did eventually sign him in 1977 for £270,000, Clough said: 'We took some stick over buying Shilton, but I would have paid twice that amount if necessary. If Trevor Francis was worth £1 million, so was Shilton. It was like buying a painting, like a Constable or a Turner. Shilton won us the First Division title the following season. He was the deciding factor and the most significant signing we (he and Peter Taylor) made by a mile. I didn't tell him, of course. One big head was enough at our club! But he was the difference. He made the fewest mistakes, and that included the management!'

Taylor added: 'We became a different side when Peter Shilton came on board. With him we had a chance. Without him, we didn't.'

The fact that Shilton helped Forest win the First Division Championship, the League Cup and two European Cups, had to be one of Bobby Robson's real regrets during his illustrious managerial career.

Felicity! Count my chickens (I'll count the sheep in the car!)

Mick Hill was a character in more ways than one. Signed by Bobby from Sheffield United for £20,000 in October 1969, the lanky striker spent just over four years at Portman Road in which time he was capped twice by Wales.

A really likeable guy, Mick was something of a complex person who had Bobby tearing his hair out on more than one occasion. He lived alone on the town's Chantry estate, living The Good Life – and yes, I mean that Good Life. The place was awash with chickens, rabbits and the like. All that was missing was a framed picture of Richard Briers and Felicity Kendal on the wall.

Timekeeping was certainly not one of Mick's assets and there were frequent occasions when I went down to Portman Road during the week and Bobby would ask me if I minded popping round to Mick's house and pick him up for training. Off I went and found Mick, as usual, feeding the chickens and tending to the wildlife. At such times he seemed to forget that he was a professional footballer, and on this occasion, obviously influenced by the surroundings, I got him into the car by telling him that Bobby was down at the ground spitting feathers.

Besides his love of poultry and lots of other of god's little creatures, Mick was a snappy dresser and his love of clothes was something else. Like the drunk who cannot pass a pub without going in for a drink, Mick couldn't pass a clothes shop without going in and buying something. His wardrobe was enormous with clothes scattered here, there and everywhere. If he could have upped his little Chantry Farm and moved it to either Carnaby Street or the King's Road then he'd have been right in his element. However, it wasn't the teeming wardrobe but the teeming outside of the property that concerned the neighbours and eventually, following complaints about his livestock, he left the rented house and went to live with Bob Shelley, a good friend and landlord to many Town players over the years, in Milton Street on the north-east side of town.

On the pitch, however, Mick did a good job for Town and scored 20 goals in his 74 appearances, but by the end of 1973 when Bobby was really making his mark on the club, Crystal Palace came in with a £70,000 offer for him A profit of £50,000 was too good for Town to turn down for a player that simply was not reliable with some of his off-the-pitch antics. (He had also been known to sleep in his car!) Palace were then managed by the colourful Malcolm Allison, definitely stiff enough opposition for Mick in the fashion stakes, and Town accepted the London club's offer. Although Mick agreed to the move, Bobby was taking no chances. He felt that his striker might simply change his mind at the last moment, or even get off the train somewhere between Ipswich and London, so chief scout Ron Gray was entrusted to deliver him to Allison in person.

Sadly Mick is no longer with us as he died in Australia some three years ago, but he will always be fondly remembered as a good player and a very likeable guy who made a refreshing change from so many footballers with all his eccentricities that you just wouldn't associate with a professional footballer from any era, but particularly today. Just imagine: Sky1 8.30pm: The Rooney's: At Home with the Chickens.

When in Rome... run!

The UEFA Cup campaign of the 1973-74 season was unforgettable for many reasons, but Wednesday 7th November sticks out in my mind because it was the night I had a really lucky escape.

Town had just booked their place in the third round in Rome's Olympic Stadium against the Italian side Lazio, following a 6-4 aggregate win. It had been an eventful night, to say the least, but for all the wrong reasons. Bobby's side had been attacked by opposing players on the pitch, while the travelling supporters had been threatened and attacked by Lazio's fans.

In the open-air press box, the English journalists were also being threatened. It was a frightening scene, but thankfully, as the situation escalated, a phone call was to save the day.

I had left England a few days before knowing that a strike by members of the National Union of Journalists, of which I was one, was a real possibility. A phone call within minutes of the final whistle from Don Simpson, the editor-in-chief, told me and fellow reporter, Tony Garnett, that we would not be required to file any stories as we were officially on strike. That call could not have been better timed. Supporters were by this time climbing into the press area, and to be honest, anything could have happened. It was relief all round as Tony and I gathered up our things and made our way into the bowels of the stadium.

We ended up with the Town players, locked and holed up in their dressing room, which was just as well as it took a couple of hours for riot police to sort out the trouble. When the all-clear signal came, we were escorted to the team coach which had been loaned to Town by Lazio during their three-day stay. The curtains were drawn, but instead of going back to the city centre hotel, the driver was instructed to take us to a restaurant on the outskirts of Rome. The reason was because a large number of Lazio supporters were waiting outside the hotel intent on making more trouble.

We eventually arrived back at the hotel around 3am, after something to eat and a few sherberts, by which time order had been restored.

The next morning we flew back to England after surviving the scariest moment during all the years I covered football. Lazio's punishment was a mere £1,500 fine and a one-year ban from European competition, a joke even back then, bearing in mind that three years earlier they had also been banned following an attack on Arsenal's players.

Privates on parade

A funny aside to that night was that David Johnson, who despite being kicked in the privates during Town's 4-0 first leg win at Portman Road, was able to take his place on the substitutes' bench in Rome. 'Jonty' came on during the second leg and scored one of the goals in a 4-2 defeat. A few days later the star striker was passing the boardroom door at Portman Road when director Harold Smith asked him how he was and whether he had fully recovered from the kicking.

'Has the injury left a scar?,' asked Harold. 'Jonty' promptly popped in, dropped his trousers and pants and placed his manhood on the boardroom table for an inspection!

The nosy director had his answer.

Close but no cigar

Holland was the next destination on this eventful European journey, where Town secured a 3-1 aggregate win over FC Twente. On landing back in England at Norwich of all places, the customs officials took great delight in making a thorough search of the Town skip. Out came shorts, shirts, boots and even jock straps. The Norwich-Ipswich rivalry even went as far as that! I had excess cigars confiscated – after all it was just a fortnight before Christmas, so presents were in mind – which had Bryan Hamilton in fits of laughter. He still reminds me of that incident even now when we see each other, but at least I get to hit back with my little funny on that score. When Town got knocked out of the competition at the quarter-final stage by Lokomotive Leipzig on penalties, my abiding memory was of non-smoker Hamilton puffing on a cigarette during the penalty shoot-out to calm his nerves.

BOBBY ROBSON

June 1974–May 1978   Dave Allard

Beat West Ham, then go forth and multiply!

MY MEMORIES of this second chapter of the Robson era start on a warm May evening following an FA Youth Cup Final. The Blues' youngsters had just beaten West Ham 2-0 in the second leg to secure a 5-1 aggregate victory.

The game itself was not all that memorable, but the reception afterwards certainly was – and a speech by chairman John Cobbold brought the house down.

Two years before Town had lifted the trophy for the first time after beating Bristol City, but on this occasion, the second leg against the Hammers was watched by a crowd of 17,000 at Portman Road. All the parents of the Ipswich boys had been invited to the club for an overnight stop and were treated to food and drink before taking their seats in the directors' box. Russell Osman, later to form a first team partnership in central defence with Terry Butcher, was among the Town youth players that night and I remember his excited father, Rex, telling me: 'What a time we're all having. What a wonderful night and what a wonderful club.'

And what a wonderful reception they had afterwards at a hotel in Copdock, just a few miles outside town.

I was keeping an eye on Bobby and when wife Elsie left her husband's side at the table for a few moments, I slipped in alongside the manager.

He looked at me and said: 'What a night, hey son, what a night. The crowd were fantastic and my young players even more remarkable.'

Bobby and I then stopped talking as the chairman, Mr John, stepped on to the stage.

'Look out lad,' said Bobby. 'Here comes the cabaret.' He was spot on.

The Old Etonian thanked a few people before getting straight to the point. He declared: 'Parents, proud parents, lend me your ears. We've brought you down here at great expense. We've put you up in a top hotel and we've fed and watered you. You've seen your sons play their part in a great triumph. Now, it's getting very late. I want you all to go to your rooms and produce another Cup winning youth side for us to celebrate in 16 years time.'

Priceless.

'What about that then Dave?' said Bobby. 'Only Mr John would make a speech like that, hey?'

When I left the hotel the chairman was in the foyer with the obligatory glass of wine and shaking hands with people. He caught sight of me and came over. 'Hello Dave. Did you like my speech? How many marks out of 10 do you give me?' he asked.

I told him I had awarded 13 out of 10. He liked that.

Just before he turned to cross the foyer, he said: 'I'm going to listen at bedroom doors tonight to make sure those parents are doing what I asked.'

Knowing him as I did, I would never put anything past Mr John.

What a man.

All strikers – prima donnas

While Mr John was always great to get on with, striker Paul Mariner was a reporter's nightmare.

The super signing from Plymouth, who was soon to make the England team after coming to Suffolk, seemed to have a great dislike of the press corps.

I once asked him for his home phone number and he curtly replied: 'No need. I've got nothing to say to you now and I won't have then.'

He once gave a V-sign to the press box after scoring a goal and a colleague of mine gave him one back, and, sadly, one of the things that I've never forgotten is that one of my most embarrassing moments travelling with Town came as a result of a fracas with this, one of our greatest all-time stars.

We were in Middlesbrough on a Tuesday night before a game with Boro' at Ayresome Park and it was here I realised how deep 'Marras' dislike of the media was. I sat down for the evening meal with a group of players, when Mariner joined us. He glared at me before going over to the manager. A rather embarrassed Town chief came over and asked me if I'd go and sit over on the other side of the room with his friend, Norfolk farmer Dick Wisden.

As I went, Bobby whispered in my ear: 'Sorry son.' Later he said: 'PM is a strange lad Dave. I'm sorry about that, but he's a key man and I need to keep him sweet.'

When I went down for breakfast the following morning, Mariner was sitting at a table on his own. I glared at him and said: 'Will it be OK if I go and sit by the window Paul?' There was no reply and he stuck his head back into his morning paper.

So there was no fond farewell from Neal Manning and me when he went to Arsenal, but having said that, we both gained a lot of pleasure from watching the play of this super centre-forward.

But at least that's all water under the bridge now, because the good news is that the story has a happy ending. After Paul finished playing, I came face to face with him in the press room at Leeds, when he was working for a radio station. He stunned me by coming over, giving me a hug and declaring: 'Dave, I was a fool in the way I treated you press lads when I was a player, you and Neal in particular. Now I'm working in the media I realise the job you have to do much more.'

We shook hands, chewed over the fat and have been mates ever since.

Lamby was at the Lincoln!

Mariner, of course, was a key man in the 1978 FA Cup Final success over Arsenal, but before I get on to a Wembley tale or two, let me reveal one from the semi-final win over West Brom at Highbury. I was at the after-match press conference when an overjoyed Robson whispered in my ear: 'You can go in the dressing room if you want son.' I did so nervously, but immediately Allan Hunter came up and said: 'Slip up to the bar and get me a large Jameson's Mr Allard.'

'OK Big Man,' I replied.

As I passed long-serving winger, Mick Lambert, I asked him how he felt and his reply was an absolute classic.

'Never mind that,' he said, 'what won the Lincoln?'

The Lincoln Handicap had been run at Doncaster that day so I told him a horse called The Hertford had triumphed in the big race. He put his head down to continue unlacing his boots and muttered: 'I knew I should have backed it.'

It was a quote I'll always remember and typical 'Lambie'. He was that sort of bloke – a true professional who always kept his feet on the ground.

Thank you God: A premonition on Wembley Way

As I was making my way up Wembley Way for the Final, I had a real surprise and a sort of premonition that today was going to be our day. All of a sudden, from out of nowhere, standing in front of me was an ardent Town fan who the day before had been released from prison after a lengthy sentence for major fraud. I had played a bit of football against him in the past, so I said: 'Blimey, how did you get here?'

With a big grin he replied: 'Dave, you didn't think I'd miss this did you? I pleaded with the parole board to let me out yesterday and they did.'

Well, I thought, if the law is on our side, then maybe the Good Lord himself is too.

And another thing. My dodgy old mate must have also had some good contacts on the outside as his seat was not far away from the Royal Box!

Little tyke!

The first man many of the sports reporters made straight for at the end of the Cup Final was, understandably, match-winner Roger Osborne.

A colleague of mine from a Sunday paper asked him where he was from and Osborne duly said 'Otley'. Naturally I knew it was a Suffolk village a few miles outside Ipswich, but this reporter made the cardinal error of assuming it to be the town of Otley in Yorkshire. The following morning the national paper had a picture of a roaring Roger jumping in the air with his top set of teeth out beneath the apt headline 'Eeee by gum,' while underneath the sub-deck read... 'Tyke Roger is Ipswich cup hero.'

Oh dear, what a blunder!

Ice cold in Chelmsford...

The celebrations at the Cup success were long and hard, but my favourite story comes from the day after the Final as the Town party travelled from their west London hotel to the civic reception in Ipswich.

Bobby agreed to a comfort stop at the Army and Navy pub in Chelmsford and more drinks were consumed as customers admired the medals the players had taken in with them.

Eventually, Bobby called time on the celebrations and everyone returned to the bus. They hadn't gone more than a hundred yards when Allan Hunter shouted: 'Stop the bus, stop the bus.'

It duly stopped and he told the manager that he had left his medal on the bar. Allan ran back to the pub but came back with a bag of ice.

He said to Bobby: 'Well boss, we'd run out of ice for the Bacardi and Coke.'

The manager, so elated by the work of his team in north London the day before, just smiled.

He later told me: 'My boys had done me so proud. On that day I couldn't deny them anything.'

...but it's a Beattie inferno!

There were all sorts of rumours flying around when, back in 1976, central defensive colossus Kevin Beattie spent a couple of weeks in hospital after suffering severe burns all over his body.

One was that his wife, Maggie, had thrown hot fat from a chip pan over him. That was complete nonsense and what's more, malicious.

Beattie has told me on numerous occasions what actually happened and his version was also backed up by Bobby Robson as well as several doctors to whom I spoke.

In a bid to liven up a fading bonfire in the garden of his Ipswich home, the England player poured petrol on to it.

It certainly did the trick and the whole thing exploded into Beattie's face and on to his body. He was rushed to hospital and Bobby told me: 'I went to see him that night and he was a terrible sight with wicked burns all over him.'

Bobby went on: 'I said "son, son, what have you done?" Kevin replied: "Boss, boss, don't worry. I'll be fit for Saturday".'

He was out for nearly two months.

BOBBY ROBSON

June 1974–May 1978   Neal Manning

It's crashing cats and dogs!

JUST three weeks before Town's 1978 FA Cup Final triumph against Arsenal, two of the squad were involved in a car crash that would have made huge headlines had it happened today. The two players, who I cannot name, wrapped a car around a lamp post in the centre of Ipswich and not only escaped the long arm of the law but also emerged virtually unscathed from the accident. Bob Shelley, that lifelong friend and fan of the club we first met helping out Mick Hill, revealed what happened that night.

He said: 'I was in the taxi office next to a café which I owned when I heard an almighty bang. I ran out into the street and saw that this car had hit a lamp post so hard it had smashed the windscreen. I soon realised that it was two Town players who were in the car. One of them had a small cut to his head, but the other one was unhurt. No one else was involved, so I decided that it would be best to get the car out of the way and pushed it into the nearby car park of a swimming pool.'

A little while later the police turned up and asked where the accident was, but Bob pleaded ignorance and then drove off with the two players – who had both been drinking – in the back of his car. He then dropped them off at their respective homes and advised them that if the matter went any further to say that a dog ran out into the road and in swerving to miss it the car hit the lamp post.

The police, however, were suspicious, and somehow found out a couple of Town players had been involved. On the Monday morning, Bobby summoned the two players to his office. He had been told that they had been involved in an accident on the Saturday night and wanted to find out the truth.

Bob Shelley said: 'I found out later that one player told Bobby that a golden retriever had run out and made them swerve, but the other one said it was a cat! Bobby was probably relieved that neither of the players were injured so near to the Final, and although he didn't believe them, he was anxious that the incident didn't make the papers. That was the end of the matter, but had it got out, it would have been very embarrassing for the club, especially at such a high profile time.'

6-1 Villa, what are the odds?

Seven days before what turned out to be that great Wembley day, Town were hit for six in their penultimate First Division match of the season. Colin Viljoen, who played in this 6-1 defeat against Aston Villa at Villa Park, became the target of 'player power' and was left out of the Cup Final line-up, with Roger Osborne, the players' choice, taking his place. Goalkeeper Paul Overton, who played his only senior game for Town in that Division One thrashing, was easily their man-of-the-match.

Afterwards, Villa manager Ron Saunders was asked if he could make a case for Ipswich winning at Wembley a week later. Saunders was adamant that Arsenal would win, at which point Tony Garnett of the *East Anglian Daily Times*, challenged the Villa manager to a bet. Saunders immediately took £20 from his pocket – a sizeable sum in those days – and sarcastically implied that would be too much money for a mere provincial journalist to match! Tony's response was to take £20 from his wallet, much to Saunders' surprise, and a Villa official put the money in an envelope and took the journalist's address should Town be successful. The money was duly posted off to Tony following Town's 1-0 Wembley triumph.

Six foot two, eyes of blue...

Allan Hunter will always be regarded as something of a legend as far as Town supporters are concerned. The Northern Ireland international, affectionately known as 'the big man', played a significant part in the club's rise under Bobby Robson. As in inscribed in club history, Allan and Kevin Beattie formed one of the best central defensive partnerships in the history of the game – and that's no exaggeration – and it was little wonder that Bobby christened them 'eggs and bacon'.

'Big Al' was a real character, but he didn't suffer fools gladly. He could be as hard as nails or a gentle giant, depending on the situation. He liked a drink and was a regular smoker – until he gave up a few years ago – but it never affected him on the pitch. On the eve of the FA Cup Final, Allan was still a doubt, and was to have a fitness test on the morning of the match.

He was de§§sperate to play, but the night before the Final, he hardly had a wink of sleep, preferring to chain-smoke his way through the small hours.

Allan took trainer Cyril Lea by surprise when he showed up bright and ready for his fitness test as early as 8am. He sailed through it, and the rest, as they say, is history.

...and Big Ron, he likes you too

Ron Atkinson was a larger-than-life manager who lost out to Bobby Robson in the 1978 FA Cup semi-final when Town beat his West Bromwich Albion side 3-1 at neutral Highbury.

I got to know Ron a couple of years earlier when he was manager of Cambridge United. Colin Harper, who was coming towards the end of his Portman Road career, had been taken on loan by Cambridge as they were pushing for promotion from the old Fourth Division during the 1976-77 season. Colin rang me one day to ask if I fancied a trip to Southend one Friday night where Cambridge were due to play. So off I went to Roots Hall with Colin to meet up with his new teammates at a hotel. After being introduced to Ron, he invited me to the pre-match meal and after the game, which Cambridge won 1-0 to boost their promotion challenge, I had a drink with Ron before driving Colin back to Ipswich. Cambridge often played on Friday nights and there were one or two other occasions when I drove Colin to matches. It also gave me the opportunity to get to know 'Big Ron' who was always good value, especially with his one-liners. Ron's status as an up-and-coming manager landed him his next job at West Brom and we still kept in touch, so when Albion drew Town in the FA Cup semi-final it meant that I would have more contact with him than usual. The week before the semi-final, instead of covering Town's match at Manchester City, I went and watched the big man's new team at Leicester, where we had arranged to meet up to do a feature on the build-up the Cup game.

Ron was a media man's dream and was particularly helpful to his local paper. After the game at Leicester he said we were going to a Greek restaurant in the city where he not only paid for the meal, but gave me enough material for a couple of page-long features. As I drove home to Ipswich that Saturday night, I couldn't help feeling that Ron was a bit over-confident about beating Robson's side, but after Town had beaten Albion and booked their place at Wembley, Ron was gracious in defeat and acknowledged that the better side had won on the day.

Wot! No dinner!

I bumped into the big man again a month later, this time on Wembley Way. It was a couple of hours after Town had beaten Arsenal on that never-to-be-forgotten May day and I was walking back to where I had parked my car.

'I suppose you're off to the celebration function Neal,' he said. I told him that I was not as the local press had not been invited, and he looked at me disbelievingly.

'You're joking,' he said. 'Every time I have taken a side to Wembley, there was always a table for the local press and radio at the after-match function.'

We shook hands, promised to stay in touch, and I was pleased when he was appointed manager of Manchester United during the summer of 1982. We hadn't seen each other since Town beat Albion, but before Ipswich went to Old Trafford for a League match in September 1982, I gave him a call. Since his appointment as United boss, I had delayed ringing him, thinking he would be far too busy with his high-profile job. When I was put through to him, Ron's first words were: 'About time too!' We talked about the forthcoming match against Town in which Arnold Muhren would be playing against his old club. After the match, which United won 3-1, Ron said to me: 'I didn't realise just how good Muhren's left foot was until he arrived here.'

Two days later Town were off to Italy to play Roma in a UEFA Cup tie and Ron's parting words to me were: 'Make sure you go to Sabbatini's when you're there.' At that time, Sabbatini's was one of the most famous fish restaurants in the world. I knew I wouldn't make it and I didn't due to a great deal of my time being taken up with the new England manager, a certain Bobby Robson, who had just left a certain Division 1 legend Mick Mills out of his squad. But that's another story.

My name is Bond – Dave Bond

My co-author Dave Allard was a dab hand at imitating certain football people. Bobby Ferguson was one and so was the then Norwich City manager, John Bond. In fact, Dave was so good at impersonating Bond that he could have put himself right in the national spotlight on terrestrial television. The offer had come came from Martin Tyler, who was then working for *ITV* but is now *Sky Sports'* chief commentator.

In those days the Town team, together with Dave and I and several supporters, used to fly to Merseyside for the games at Everton and Liverpool. On this particular occasion, around the dinner table at the Holiday Inn Hotel, Dave started doing his John Bond impressions. Martin was so impressed that he wanted him to appear on a show that *ITV* were putting together for Christmas, but Dave got stage fright. Despite me telling him he should grab the opportunity – plus I'd told Martin that I was his agent! – Dave wouldn't budge and the nation lost the chance of seeing a great act.

BOBBY ROBSON

June 1978–May 1982   Dave Allard

Aberdeen Alex

THE trip to Alex Ferguson's Aberdeen in the first, and last, defence of the UEFA Cup by Town is a football adventure I will never forget.

The result was a dismal one for Ipswich as they lost 3-1 after being held 1-1 at Portman Road. The venture to the Granite City, though, was special for me in that I got to know Ferguson. And to the great man's credit, when I've met him down the years since, he's always recognised me and stopped to have a chat, the last time being on the sad occasion of Sir Bobby's memorial service reception in Durham.

But back to that night and, apart from the result, the other maybe even more unpleasant memory of that trip was the horrific virus that engulfed – yes, engulfed – Neal Manning. Now, I'll leave it to your imagination, but cover keeper John Jackson tagged the situation at the team hotel as 'The H-Block Protest!' But at least he wasn't without his visitors. Jimmy Leadbetter, Town's wing legend from the Alf Ramsey era, came up from his Edinburgh home for the game and as he knew Neal well, he visited his room to have a chat. You could tell how bad Neal was as the following morning he said to me: 'Do you know what? I had a dream last night. I dreamt Jimmy Leadbetter was at the foot of my bed.' Oh dear.

We had flown from Southend to the Dyce Airport just outside Aberdeen and Neal had been able to come down to Pittodrie Park for the training session the night before the match. With us was Jimmy Barker, a regular Town 'Euro traveller' and all three of us stood behind the goal watching the Ipswich players go through their paces under boss Robson and coach Bobby Ferguson.

Suddenly, a voice behind us boomed out: 'Good evening boys.'

We looked round and there was Dons' chief Ferguson leaning on a crash barrier. Neal and I had got to know him a bit during the first leg in Suffolk and his willingness to talk to us and general friendliness was most impressive. Now here he was, hopping over the wall from the terraces, to say: 'Come up to the office for a drink.' We were there like a shot.

'What's your poison chaps?' inquired the ex-Rangers striker and ex-Govan shipyard worker. We all had lagers, while Alex poured himself a Bacardi and coke.

We thought he was going to quiz us about Town, but nothing could have been further from the truth as all he wanted to do was to chat and exchange banter. And so much so that by the time we piled into a taxi outside Pittodrie, we were all as well oiled as the rigs off the coast. And Alex even came down to the club reception to wave us off. 'Jump in boys and see you tomorrow night. By the way, the cab's paid for. It's on Aberdeen Football Club's account.'

Poor Neal failed to make the match – one to miss given the result – as the virus by this stage had struck with full force, so the aforementioned Jimmy, who owned a Suffolk scaffolding company, was enlisted to help me at the game and delighted in collecting quotes after the match as I prepared stories for both the *EADT* and *Evening Star. I remember he* came back up to the press box with quotes and stressed: 'Alex Ferguson says we must go to his office before we leave.' So after getting the *EADT* reports done, I decided to leave the *Star* stories for telephoning the following morning before breakfast in order to leave time to see the host manager.

We climbed the stairs to Alex's office where the victorious manager was drinking with coach Archie Knox, other members of his staff, family and friends.

'Dave, Jimmy, come in boys',' he said as we got to the door and he also enquired as to Neal's whereabouts.

'He's being given the last rites back at the hotel,' laughed Jimmy.

During our stay there was no mention about the game that had just been played as all that had been discussed earlier. Alex and Archie told stories, as did Jimmy and I, on a night I shall never forget.

Miss World and Mr Universe

Not long after that match, there was a happier occasion for Bobby when an England XI came to Portman Road in November 1979 for his testimonial match. The star turn in the Blues line-up was a certain George Best, who, going along with legend, Bobby had operating in the number seven shirt.

The former Manchester United mega-icon may have been getting slightly portly, but he still thrilled the fans and delighted many Portman Road folk with a bit of inside information, which, typically, had nothing to do with the football. Best, who had courted the 1977 Miss World winner, Mary Stavin of Sweden, predicted that Gina

Swainson of Bermuda would win the beauty contest which, at the time, was still two weeks away. And he didn't just predict it, he absolutely insisted on it, and, needless to say, as a result many Town players got their money on early at big odds. And the aging footballing maestro and beauty queen love god proved to be spot on with his prediction when the 21-year-old won the title in London on 15th November and as a result a lot of people cleaned up, which, with all due respect to Bobby, was just the testimonial they were looking for.

I bet my Bondy beats your Bondy

In January 1980 snow and ice gripped East Anglia and pitches were frozen.

Neal and I were sitting in our office one Wednesday morning when Bobby rang to say: 'Come with us to the seaside, chaps.' Before adding: 'I've arranged with Ken Brown at Norwich for us to play each other on a frost free pitch at Yarmouth.'

Neal and I went off with the squad up the A12 with our destination being Yarmouth's Wellesley Road ground. At the time, I was noted for doing a rather good impression of former Norwich chief John Bond and following his appointment to Manchester City, Ken was moved up from his role as assistant manager to replace him.

I was having a cup of coffee in the supporters' lounge before the game, when a beaming Ken came in.

'Mr Allard, Mr Allard, the very man,' I recall him saying.

With Neal alongside him, he went on: 'There's a big competition in prospect in our dressing room and you are required.'

Now, you've just heard from Neal how my route to Mike Yarwood superstardom was blocked only by a cruel bout of stage fright, but on this more minor occasion I had no such problem. It transpired that Canaries' left-back Greg Downs was also renowned for his Bond take-off and Ken's plan was for Greg and I to give our versions in front of the City squad.

Brown added: 'The lads will judge who is best at it.'

Bobby Robson stood laughing in the City dressing room doorway as Brown announced Greg and me before we did our bits.

I'm too modest to say who won, but suffice to say, Greg declared: 'You sound more like Bondy than Bondy.'

City striker John Deehan, later to become a Town player, was the real hero of the day and scored four goals as City won 5-1.

To end where it all began

The much-acclaimed Robson era came to an end in the summer of 1982 and I was determined to mark it with something very different, so photographer David Kindred and I came up with an idea. The picture of the 39-year-old Robson at Ipswich Station in 1969 with Johnny Cobbold, chauffer Roger Nightingale, and the car of course, was brought out of mothballs. Our plan was to set the same picture up 13 years on from his arrival. Mr John and Roger were happy so I then contacted the man of the moment.

'Great idea son,' said Bobby. 'Come and pick me up when you're ready.'

So I set it up and took Bobby to the station where David arranged the picture just as it was 13 years before. Mr John said typically as he shook Bobby's hand: 'Piss off Robson, piss off. Go and leave us, go on.' The laughter rang out all round, but everyone's eyes watered, including mine. I could see that Bobby was particularly choked when I took him back to the ground.

So I changed the subject and asked him to tell me another story about Bobby Keetch, his room-mate during playing days at Fulham. Keetch was a terrific character in so many ways and the Town chief often told me about his exploits.

'What about this one son,' said Bobby and off he went on a 'Keetchy' tale.

It was such a long one that he was 10 minutes in the car at the ground before he went up to his office.

But despite the stories, Bobby was hurting. It was heartbreaking for him to be leaving the club he loved so much.

BOBBY ROBSON

June 1978–May 1982   Neal Manning

Nice one Cyril, and Bobby's only human

CYRIL LEA, first signed by Bill McGarry from Leyton Orient, had served Ipswich Town as player, caretaker manager and first team coach for almost 15 years, but just before the start of the 1979-80 season, Cyril left Portman Road to become assistant-manager to Alan Durban at Stoke City, and it was the departure of this long serving club favourite that led to Bobby Robson and I having a public bust-up. The row had been simmering for a few weeks and eventually boiled over after Cyril's first return to his old stamping ground in only the fourth match of the season when Town beat Stoke in a First Division match.

Robson had said that Cyril had left by mutual consent with Bobby Ferguson being promoted from the reserves to take over as first team coach. Cyril, however, categorically denied this and told me he had been sacked, something he felt had been on the cards for some time because Robson very much wanted Ferguson as his number two. The former Welsh international and I had been friends for a long time, playing golf and/or having a few drinks on many occasions.

On the eve of Town's match against Stoke in early September, Dave and I went to see Cyril for a drink at the Potteries' club's overnight hotel. We talked for several hours and told him that he could expect a big reception from the Town fans the following afternoon. And that is certainly what he got. Even former Town chairman John Cobbold took his place in the directors' box earlier than normal to clap and show his appreciation.

In the week leading up to Cyril's return, Robson had been strangely unavailable, not even answering his phone. With little news coming out of Portman Road, the build-up had been centred around Stoke and, of course, Cyril coming back just weeks after leaving. Although there was to be no fairytale ending to the trip for Cyril or his new club, Robson was gunning for a row. Among the accusations from the Town manager were that I wanted Stoke to win, something which I vehemently denied.

In the end, with neither of us prepared to concede any ground, Robson suddenly announced that in future there would only be a press conference once a week. What this was meant to achieve I had no idea. The freelance journalists made hay as anything Robson said became public almost immediately, while it was not until the next day that any news could be published in either the *East Anglian Daily Times* or *Evening Star.* Common sense, however, prevailed in the end. There were, in fact, only two 'weekly' press conferences before everything returned to normal.

In fact, it was the intervention of John Cobbold, who was disappointed at Cyril's departure, which played a big part in ending what was in danger of turning into something of a farce.

Mr John, who once famously said that the only crisis at the club would be if the white wine ran out in the boardroom, was certainly no fool and he later told me that he'd had a quiet word with his manager about his lack of PR sense.

Bobby and I never fell out over Cyril's return in Stoke colours. We had both had our say in front of other journalists and several club officials, but that was the end of the matter – at least by a fortnight later when we had got those two 'weekly' press conferences out of the way.

Credit to the other Bobby

With the growing success of the club under his tenure Bobby inevitably changed somewhat over time. Sometimes it did seem that a touch of arrogance got the better of him. In the early days of his Portman Road reign, he was never afraid to seek advice as he started to lay the foundations for the many years of success the club was to enjoy, but by the time Cyril left, the club had enjoyed several years of European competition as well as winning the FA Cup, so I suppose it was inevitable that there were to be times when he felt he could do nothing wrong and that he was above criticism. He always liked to take the credit – and most of the time he was justified in doing so – but I can recall an occasion when I wrote a story in which Bobby Ferguson took the headlines. It was in Town's UEFA Cup winning run of 1980-81 when they were drawn against the Polish side Widzew Lodz in the third round.

Ferguson went on a spying trip to Poland before the first leg at Portman Road. Widzew Lodz had beaten both Juventus and Manchester United in previous rounds and were obviously a very good side, but Ferguson came back from Poland convinced Town could beat them. Tactically he got it spot on as the Blues romped to a 5-0 victory.

I wrote a story to this effect, but it did not go down well with Robson. His loyal secretary Pat Godbold used to collect all press cuttings referring to the manager and pass them on to him.

It was just another spat we had, but again was soon forgotten. What I will say is that considering I was reporting on the club's fortunes for the whole of his 13-year reign, the odd fall-out was inevitable, but generally our relationship was harmonious. In fact, he was a great help on so many occasions. Bobby was always prepared to give of his time even though he was living life very much in the fast lane as he turned the unfashionable Suffolk club into one of best in Europe. And when his country came calling, it was inevitable that he would move on. It was certainly an end of an era and the club has never been the same since.

So good we paid it twice

In those halcyon days of the 1970s and early '80s, Town often took to the air to get to matches. With such a heavy programme, when they played at the likes of Everton and Liverpool the club wanted to save the players from long and tiring coach journeys. And usually, to offset the cost of hiring the plane, the club took a number of supporters, mainly the successful businessmen of the town.

I remember one such occasion when we flew from Southend to Speke airport on Merseyside for a Saturday match against Everton at Goodison Park. After dinner at the team's hotel on the Friday evening, it was time to hit the Liverpool night life. Regulars on these plane trips were well known Suffolk characters like Ken Bean, Bob Shelley, Charlie Manning, Horace Chilvers, Gerald Milsom, Dick Wisden and Roy Davies, who was also Alan Brazil's father-in-law.

On this occasion we all piled into a club and the champagne started to flow. The local Liverpool girls were well impressed and it was an evening full of laughs.

On the coach to the ground the next day, somebody asked who paid the bill and how much did we owe. Roy Davies said he paid £200 (a lot of money in those days), and the night was on him but seconds later Bob Shelley said that he had also paid the same bill, not realising that Roy had settled it! No wonder Town supporters were always very welcome guests on Merseyside in the future!

Let's be Frank – I was man of the match

Frank McLintock was captain of Arsenal's double winning side that was managed by Bertie Mee in 1971. A decade later I had the privilege of playing alongside him in a match in Amsterdam the day before the UEFA Cup Final between Ipswich and AZ '67 Alkmaar.

For several years Phil Houseley and I used to organise matches between the British Press and the press of the country in which Town were playing a European game. Phil and his brother David ran Felixstowe Travel, the company responsible for organising Town supporters' trips abroad with such resounding success.

The British Press team was often boosted by Bobby Robson, Cyril Lea and Bobby Ferguson, and all three played in Innsbruck on a most scenic and memorable ground set in the mountains.

Two years before the UEFA Cup Final triumph, Town had met AZ '67 Alkmaar in the first round of the European Cup Winners Cup, and the day before the tie we had a press match.

Ipswich had brought three goalkeepers to Holland for that game and being short of a 'keeper on this occasion, I asked Bobby Robson if Kieron Baker could play as he was not going to be involved in the main event. Bobby said yes and Kieron kept a clean sheet as Phil scored the only goal to give us victory. Our reward was that each player was presented with a large Dutch cheese.

In Oslo back in 1979 we took a 6-0 hammering from a Norwegian team that included a player who had played for Lillestrom against Glasgow Rangers in the European Cup only the previous week!

Whenever there was an opportunity Phil and I put out a side that often included two of Fleet Street's finest, Brian Scovell (*Daily Mail*) and Brian Woolnough (then *The Sun*). Stuart Jarrold (then Anglia TV) and Peter Barraclough (then Radio Orwell) also played in many of the games.

But my abiding memory is of that far flung afternoon in Amsterdam when we had a terrific 2-2 draw against a strong Dutch Press side. I had a good game that day and was particularly thrilled when Frank McLintock sung my praises and made me man of the match.

Mills across the Mersey

It was like a scene from a James Bond film, but it was no joke as far as Town's record-breaking captain Mick Mills was concerned. In December 1981 Town had travelled to Merseyside for a League Cup fourth round tie against Everton.

It was there that Bobby Robson revealed to Dave Allard and me that Mick could no longer be guaranteed a place in the side as he pointed to the emergence of Irvin Gernon.

I must say it took us very much by surprise. Nobody is irreplaceable in life, but Millsy came close. Since arriving in Suffolk in 1966 after Portsmouth had disbanded their youth scheme, he had made a massive contribution to the club.

On the morning of the Everton tie, Mick, Dave and I made the short trip through the Mersey Tunnel to go and see former Town midfielder Bryan Hamilton who was then the manager of Tranmere Rovers. It was *en route* that the drama unfolded as we were suddenly aware our taxi was being followed by a limousine with blacked out windows.

We didn't think too much about it as we spent that hour of so with Bryan, but on the journey back, the same car followed us back to the hotel. As we pulled up and were paying the fare, the driver of the limousine tapped on the window and said to Mick: 'There are a couple of Sunderland directors who would like to speak to you.' What Robson had told Dave and I earlier had obviously moved on quickly, and we began to wonder if this had been pre-arranged. Why would Sunderland's representatives be on Merseyside when there had not been an inkling that Town might be preparing to sell their captain?

Mills refused to talk to the Sunderland duo, but had obviously been taken by surprise that his days at Portman Road might be numbered. Despite me saying he had nothing to lose by having a chat, Mick was adamant he would not speak to them. Surprise, anger and a host of other emotions were going through the captain's mind.

The Sunderland board members were not impressed at being snubbed but they were not to get their man. A few months late Mick was to captain his country at the 1982 World Cup Finals in Spain, but before the end of that year his long Town reign was over, and in the December he joined Southampton during Bobby Ferguson's first season in charge after Robson left to take over as manager of England.

Jesus John!

There was never a dull moment if you were in the company of the Cobbold brothers. Over the years I had spent many hours with either John or Patrick, or both, at home and abroad and on this particular occasion a trip to Luton for an FA Cup fourth round tie in January 1982, comes readily to mind.

A few days before the Luton game, Dave Allard and I were having a drink with the Cobbolds and they asked us how we were travelling to Luton.

We told them that local businessman Bob Shelley, who knew them both, was driving us, and they asked us if they could have a lift. We met at Portman Road with John immediately saying: 'It should be fun travelling in a Mafia staff car!', a reference to Bob with his Maltese looks.

As we were leaving Ipswich, a car carved us up on a roundabout and almost hit the front passenger side where Patrick was sitting. The immediate response from John was: 'I nearly got my old job back,' referring to the fact that Patrick was now chairman.

We stopped for lunch at a hotel just outside Luton where to John and Patrick's dismay they only had half bottles of wine.

Not to be deterred, John got on the phone to an Old Etonian friend of his who just happened to be the chairman of the company who owned the hotel. The upshot was that one of the staff was sent out to get full bottles of wine. Problem solved!

Rest in peace – and send flowers

An article I wrote towards the end of the 1979-80 season had Bobby Robson spitting feathers. The headline read: 'RIP Ipswich Town. Send flowers to...'

It had come about after Town were going to miss out once again on the chance of winning the First Division title. The club had been in so many good positions of winning the title that Bobby badly wanted, but it seemed another opportunity was lost. As soon as the paper hit the streets, Bobby was on the phone saying that the club was not dead.

I had pointed out that a couple of signings before the transfer deadline might have helped and also there was not sufficient strength in depth in the squad. I must have been on the phone to him for at least an hour and after having my ears pinned back, I was eventually able to calm him down.

I did admit that possibly I had gone a bit over the top, but in the end we finished airing our differences of opinion and that was the end of the matter. For the record, Town finished third that season behind Liverpool and Manchester United – and that was deemed to be a failure! How times have changed since.

BOBBY FERGUSON

July 1982–May 1987   Neal Manning

Wrong dressing room, right result

MONDAY 7th May 1984 was a pivotal day in the club's history with a victory over Manchester United at Old Trafford guaranteeing their First Division safety.

But for Bobby Ferguson, in his second season in charge after taking over from Bobby Robson, there was a definitive moment that perhaps helped Town gain the result they so badly needed.

About an hour before kick-off, Bobby, Dave and I were having a cigarette standing by the directors' box. Dave and I were doing our best to keep him calm, but Bobby was understandably very nervous in view of what was riding on the game. Soon he went off to see his players to tell them the United line-up and we watched him walk down the corridor reading the team sheet before going into the dressing room. Sadly for him it was the wrong one! The first person he thought he saw was Romeo Zondervan, when in fact it was Remi Moses.

Realising his mistake, Bobby beat a hasty retreat and went to the Town dressing room and told the players what he had just done. They all laughed – and so did Ferguson at his own faux pas.

Mich D'Avray, who scored the first goal in a 2-1 victory, recalled how it had lifted the tension and the players took to the pitch relaxed and with a spring in their step. Happily, victory over Aston Villa in the next and final match of the season catapulted Town up to a finishing position of 12th that only a few weeks earlier had seemed impossible. For Ferguson it had been a remarkable triumph. Had Town been relegated that season, it would not have been a surprise considering what had happened during the campaign. Even an experienced manager like Bobby Robson would have been severely tested given the same circumstances, but for Ferguson he had had to take blow after blow on the chin.

Firstly, there had been the death of former chairman John Cobbold at the age of only 56. A month later Paul Mariner and John Wark both demanded big pay rises and told the club if they didn't get them they wanted transfers. Their pay demands were refused and the disgruntled players stayed for the time being.

Just to add to an increasingly frustrating season, Town were dumped out of the FA Cup by Third Division Shrewsbury Town, and within 48 hours I revealed in *The Evening Star* that the club were £1.6 million in debt – peanuts today but quite a bit then. Among many supporters the news was met with disbelief and some senior officials at the club tried to deny it but I knew I was on safe ground. I had been given the facts chapter and verse by a boardroom contact the day after the Shrewsbury defeat.

Within a month Bobby had been forced to sell Mariner to Arsenal for a paltry £140,000 to pay a tax bill, while Wark went to Liverpool for £450,000 to help reduce the overall debt.

Seven consecutive defeats followed that made Town odds-on favourites to be relegated, but much credit must go to Bobby in that the club finished the season on a real high with five wins and two draws – including one against

Liverpool at Anfield – to take them to that almost unbelievable 12th place finish.

Relegation eventually came three seasons later after defeat against Charlton in the play-offs, but for Fergie it had been a struggle from the day he took over from Robson. He had been under pressure from virtually day one of his five-year reign as manager. The great team that had won the UEFA Cup in 1981 and, in fact, came close to completing the treble of the First Division Championship, FA Cup and the European triumph, was starting to break up. Besides Mariner and Wark, Mick Mills, Alan Brazil and the two Dutch masters, Frans Thijssen and Arnold Muhren, left in Ferguson's first season in charge, but there was still enough quality in the team for him to steer the club to a ninth place finish.

Dethroned in Italy

Talking of Mills, I shall now reveal the story I alluded to during one of the sections on Bobby Robson.

Three months after captaining his country in the 1982 World Cup Finals in Spain, Mick was left out of the first England squad picked by his former club manager, Bobby Robson. While shocked by his omission, the timing of the announcement could not have been worse for Town as it came on the eve of their UEFA Cup first round, first leg tie against Roma in Italy.

The Town skipper was preparing for what proved to be the club's last participation in Europe for 15 years – after the home leg a fortnight later – when he heard the news.

What I had anticipated as a quiet day, with just a preview to write and phone, turned out to be a busy one. The previous Saturday, while at Old Trafford for a First

Division match against Manchester United, their manager Ron Atkinson had told me that when in Italy to make sure I went to Sabbatini's, then a world-renowned fish restaurant.

That all went out of the window once the news of Mick being dropped from the England squad came through. While the rest of the Town players relaxed with a sightseeing trip, he chose to stay at the hotel.

I went to his room to get his reaction to the news and understandably he was far from pleased. However, like he had been all the years I had known him, he gave me some great copy.

I then sat down by the hotel swimming pool to write my story – taking a swim from time to time to cool off – before phoning it through to catch the later editions of the *Evening Star.*

A 3-0 defeat against Roma the following night made it a thoroughly miserable trip for Town, and Mills in particular. Goalkeeper Paul Cooper had a nightmare and was badly at fault for two of the goals. Bobby Ferguson was so angry with Cooper – I can't repeat some of his comments – but the outcome was that he was dropped for Town's next game against Stoke three days later.

Chalk and cheese, not eggs and bacon

Fergie was altogether a different personality to Robson. As a combination they had been as good as any, but it was a different story when Bobby number two became Bobby number one. Events off the field certainly didn't help, but whereas Robson was the diplomat and a master at man-management, the same could not be said of his successor. He was a much more abrasive character and was never afraid of upsetting people he thought knew nothing about the game. So although, for the most part, I found him very approachable and helpful, there were inevitably times when he would fly off the handle and have a real go if he didn't agree with something I wrote.

And given his natural temperament it was no great revelation to find that when it came to the public relations side of the job, Bobby left a great deal to be desired. Robson, on the other hand, in his time at Ipswich, had become a master at the PR game. He knew what journalists wanted and he had many friends in Fleet Street. The London-based writers used to love coming to Portman Road because the ever more successful manager so often took centre stage after matches and the hospitality was second to none. Indeed between them Bobby Robson and John Bond made East Anglia the most hospitable footballing area in the country back then. John also knew all that he needed to know about making his football club a great place for journalists. There were many occasions – especially after midweek matches at Carrow Road – when Dave and I would not get home until 4am. John used to take over the boardroom and then it was off to a restaurant in the city for a late night meal. Ah, no wonder a fella can get to miss the good old days!

Dig the new breed!

But I digress. Back to Fergie. I remember going to his office after I had written the story about the club being in debt. It had obviously put more pressure on him, although to be fair it was nothing to do with him. His hand had been forced by the club's overspending in recent years. After the Cup defeat by Shrewsbury, coupled with the League form, there was obviously gloom and doom among the supporters, so all in all Bobby had picked an interesting moment to include 15-year-old schoolboy Jason Dozzell in his squad for the first time for the visit of Coventry City, but, maybe a little nervously, wanted to keep it under wraps. But I argued with him that the Chantry schoolboy's inclusion in the squad should be published to try to ensure a decent crowd.

I also remember him saying: 'Coventry will come here and string a washing line across the pitch and make no attempt to attack.'

'Bob, if you want to get a crowd here on Saturday, it's no use saying things like that,' I told him. 'Get Dozzell's name in the paper, it can only help.' Eventually he saw reason but as it was there was only a crowd of just over 13,000. Jason came on as substitute and scored in a 3-1 win that certainly justified the decision to gamble with someone so young.

Food fight!

In the days before team coaches had microwaves and chefs on board, Town used to stop at a hotel on their way back from long trips. The Post House at Stoke-under-Lyne was the favourite stopping point after playing in the north-west, while The George in the Lincolnshire town of Stamford was the destination when heading down the A1 from the north-east. For years various Town teams had stopped there for dinner, but that all finished in the early-to-mid 1980s following a match at Sunderland.

Fergie had stayed up in the north-east following the Sunderland match to spend some time with his family and while the cat was away, the mice certainly played.

On this occasion the Town directors, who had travelled with the team, didn't have a meal and instead headed for the bar, blissfully unaware of what was going on in the room set aside for the rest of the party that included a certain Mr Allard and me. It turned into absolute carnage as several players, many of them established internationals, behaved appallingly. Staff were abused, bread rolls were thrown about the room and a fight threatened to break out after one player took offence following some mickey-taking from one of his colleagues. It was a situation totally out of control.

To be fair, it was out of character for some of the players involved, but it was not was expected from representatives of a First Division football club. The incident put Dave and me in an awkward position because we knew Bobby would want us to tell him what went on once the news filtered through. The hotel had understandably made a strong complaint and also added that the club would not be welcome in the future.

On the Monday we got the phone call we expected from Bobby asking us to see him and, without naming names, we told him what had happened. The manager's job was hard enough without an embarrassing incident like this. One thing is for sure though. Such an incident would not have occurred had Bobby been there.

Generally par, but the odd bogey

If you could get Bobby away from football, he was good company, despite the fact that he could never completely relax.

I played golf with him at Ipswich Golf Club at Purdis Heath on many occasions. He is still a member there and has always been more than a useful player.

On an afternoon – when there were seldom many people on the course – he and I used get round in sometimes just over two hours. That's the way he liked to play and he was none too happy if he was held up by slow players. On away trips, when he was coach to Bobby Robson, he was very chatty, but he never forgot that he had a job to do and for that reason relaxing was not in his vocabulary. He occasionally came round to my house for a drink and twice came to parties – as did some of the players, but once he became manager, I knew things would change. The additional pressures he had forced upon him did not help.

In the circumstances, he did a fine job in his five years at the helm. Our relationship from a work point of view continued relatively smoothly, although, that said there was one other sizable explosion when we had a huge slanging match over an article I wrote suggesting that Mick Mills, then at Stoke, was on the verge of being appointed Town's manager. Back in 1985 I had been tipped off that Bobby's job was in the balance and that if he went Mills was the man to whom the club might turn. As it turned out, that was not the case, but Bobby did not forget that one too quickly and our relationship became distinctly uneasy for a while.

Great coach and master tactician

Looking back, there is no doubt that the Robson-Ferguson combination was one of the most successful in the history of the English game. They bounced off each other perfectly and it is no coincidence that they were together when the club enjoyed the most successful period in their history. Winning both the FA Cup and the UEFA Cup in three years when Town were one of the giants of the English and European game is testimony to their partnership. Fergie was certainly not everybody's cup of tea, but he was an excellent coach – although one or two players have since said that he destroyed them – and his tactical knowledge was spot on. Two other examples, which arguably top his Widzev Lodz reconnaissance mission, come to mind. Firstly, he was fundamental to Eric Gates' success at the club by persuading Robson that his best position was 'in the hole' behind the main strikers, a tactic that worked to perfection. And secondly, in the FA Cup Final, his recommendation that Paul Mariner should play on his own up front while the pace of David Geddis down the right hand side would trouble the Gunners' left-back Sammy Nelson, was a masterstroke which helped bring the club it's most famous piece of silverware. So in short, he may have upset a few and not been too interested in launching too many charm offences but he has rightly earned his place in the club's history.

BOBBY FERGUSON

July 1982–May 1987   Dave Allard

Mind the mire down memory lane

THE Ipswich board asked Bobby Robson who should take over from him and the ball was firmly in his court. Ferguson, the trusted coach and tactical mastermind of the Robson era, had done such a good job as number two, so Robson gave his faithful lieutenant the nod and the board drank a toast to it with the two of them. I say 'faithful lieutenant' because, not many years before, Fergie had rejected the chance to take a four-year contract as manager of Millwall. He had talks at the Den and seriously considered it, but Robson got him in his office at Portman Road and offered him a five-year deal to stay as his number two. He duly accepted a job that was something of a poisoned chalice at the time, what with the club having huge payments to make on their new Britannia Stand.

Apart from the odd flashpoint, I got on well with him when he was coach. He was always helpful and good company, but while the no-nonsense Geordie did not suffer fools gladly, deep down he was quite a caring man. I have to admit though, I got off to a rather bad start with the new boss and it was all over a few 'memory lane' pictures.

When he was appointed manager, I thought I would write a little surprise *This Is Your Life* piece. One morning, when Bobby was at the ground, I went round to his house to see his wife Ann and asked for some pictures from his past. Ann got the photo albums out and I gathered pictures of her husband in Newcastle, Derby and Cardiff colours. I thought they would help to illustrate the piece and make it special for him, but I was in for a shock the day after the article was published in *The Evening Star* and *East Anglian Daily Times*.

The new manager confronted me at the ground's Centre Spot restaurant and accused me of 'being a burglar'. He said: 'You took advantage of my wife's kindness. You should have asked me first before taking those pictures.'

I then said: 'Did you like the piece I wrote?'

Bobby replied: 'Yes, it was fine.'

I came back with: 'So why are you moaning?'

Bobby exclaimed: 'Enough said. I'll speak to you tomorrow.'

Sure enough, I was on the phone to him the following day and he was as helpful, informative and cheerful as ever.

Hang out your washing on the Mark Grew line

Bobby was a good friend to me when he was coach, still a good friend when he was manager and still a good friend after he left the club, but one other flashpoint I can clearly remember was when I did an interview with keeper Mark Grew. The manager decided to spring a surprise before an old First Division trip to Oxford. First choice goalie Paul Cooper was injured and Bobby announced that he was playing rookie Jon Hallworth and not the vastly experienced Grew. On the Friday afternoon before the Saturday game at the Manor Ground, I went to see Grew at the shop he owned jointly with teammate Trevor Putney. Mark didn't hold back. He said: 'Fergie has it in for me Dave. The washing ladies have more chance of playing in goal than me.'

What happened the following day in the varsity city stunned everyone who saw it. Town were 3-0 up and looking set to get three crucial points in their relegation battle. However, after the interval, poor Hallworth had a dreadful experience as the home side roared back to win 4-3 with John Aldridge getting a hat-trick. Bobby said to me afterwards: 'If you blame young Jon Hallworth for that defeat I'll be livid.' I wasn't so much worried about that comment, but more concerned about what he would say when he read in Saturday's *Evening Star* what Grew had said.

The 'washing ladies' comment was splashed big across the back page.

I knew the balloon would go up and on Sunday morning Bobby phoned me to declare: 'Allard, let me tell you this. The washing ladies have as much chance of getting in the team as you have of getting into our ground.'

He then put the phone down.

On the Monday morning I phoned the kit room at the club to speak to the two washing ladies and apologised to them, hoping Grew's comment had not caused offence. They were fine, but I knew I had to steer clear of the manager for a few days.

By the Thursday though, I decided to break the ice. I went on to Ferguson and it was business as usual as he made no mention of the 'washing ladies' story.

Smells like team spirit

Keeper Paul Cooper once said to me: 'For Fergie to keep us up is like trying to eat your dinner with one hand tied behind your back.' But despite the gradual break up of the glory team and the big payments on the new stand, for three seasons the ex-Newcastle, Derby and Cardiff defender did keep the crestfallen Blues in the top flight.

Now and again he'd blow his top with me to create a bit of fun for onlookers and one such incident came after a 1-0 home win over Tottenham. It was a game in which his teenaged midfield duo of Jason Dozzell and Mark Brennan were outstanding. Bobby called them his 'babies' and 'the future of our club'.

Now, in a build-up to the Spurs game, a colleague of mine had written that the team lacked spirit. I won't say who it was, but it wasn't me. Bobby, however, had been told it was me.

I had always praised the spirit of the side at the time, but the Town manager came to the press room itching to have a go at me about this 'lack of spirit' business. He burst into the media room, escorted by an official, and immediately came up to me and got me by the sleeve.

'I want to see you outside,' he demanded as he pulled strongly.

I refused to go and Phil Osborn of the *Daily Express* ordered: 'Calm down Bobby. We need you here, not outside conducting a private conversation.'

In his oratory about the match, Bobby kept mentioning how good the team spirit was. After the last question he left the press room without further words with me. First team coach Charlie Woods got to hear about the 'no spirit' business and phoned me at home on the Saturday night to say: 'Look Dave, it clearly wasn't you who wrote we lacked spirit. I've impressed that several times on Bobby now and he's calmed down a bit.' And thankfully he had, as things were back to normal when I rang him on the Monday morning, but one national daily newspaper led their match report by declaring there had been a public spat between the Ipswich manager and a journalist.

But while he had a short fuse on occasions, he was a brilliant coach of footballers.

Paul Mariner came to the club from Plymouth on Bobby's strong recommendation and although the pair had their rows during the latter's coaching and managerial times, Paul has told me many times that 'Fergie was the best coach you could ever wish to work with'.

That comment has been echoed by many who worked under him and his work for Ipswich Town at all levels was immense. And it has to be remembered that he loved a good laugh too and could be great company. Arsenal and England marksman Alan Sunderland once came and stayed with me for a time following a domestic problem and during that time I hit the sports pages of the *East Anglian Daily Times* and *Evening Star* with exclusives galore.

It puzzled Bobby how I was getting so many stories before he had given them out.

Years later when I told him he was highly amused.

Easy like 'Sundy' morning, ...noon ...and night!

I once had an FA Cup Final matchwinner as a lodger – Alan Sunderland. The striker, who scored the clincher when Arsenal beat Manchester United 3-2 in the 1979 Final, was a key man up front for Ferguson's Blues.

'Sundy' and I had always got on well and one Saturday night when we were coming back from a match on the team bus, he came and sat with me and asked if he could stay at my home for a few days, saying he needed a bit of time away from his wife, Chris. I told him that he had three children and that he should stay and dig his heels in, but he was desperate for a temporary sanctuary.

I was living on my own and eventually gave in to him. We spent a lot of time on the course at Rushmere Golf Club and, as you might expect, often had a few beers together afterwards. I'd get up early to go to work in the *Evening Star* sports room in the mornings and, very handily, was well armed with all the club news 'Sundy' had told me the night before.

I was so on the ball that Ferguson said several times: 'You're incredible you are Allard. How did you know that?' I often replied: 'That's for me to know Bobby and for you to find out.'

Many years later, when I told him that 'Sundy' was my lodger, he laughed and laughed. 'Sundy' wanted to keep his new location secret, but unfortunately all the children in the street got to find out. At night they'd stand outside the house and chant his name before ringing the door bell in a bid to get his autograph.

JOHN DUNCAN

Dave Allard

He always calls you boy...

WHEN John Duncan got out of his car to walk to the Town's main office entrance on his first day as manager, I was there to meet him. He immediately recognised me as I'd been hanging around when he came down for his job interview. Before I could get a word out he said: 'You can help me boy and I can help you.' And that's exactly how it was for all his three years in charge.

I may have upset him a few times with stories I wrote, but John always put a brave face on it and said: 'You have your job boy and you have to do it, just as I have to do mine.'

Whenever I could help John I would and he was always available at the end of the phone for me. If I hadn't phoned him by half past eight in the morning at his Capel St Mary home, he'd be worried.

Now and again, I'd catch him in the bathroom, but he'd always talk.

One morning he said: 'Hang on a second boy. I've just dropped some toothpaste on the phone.'

...but this one was a dog

On the team bus, John was always involved in the front section card schools and quizzes, the front section being for management, directors and members of the press. Also, John, Bryan Knights of *BBC Radio Suffolk*, and I often used to go for a quiet drink after matches. The venue was usually a country pub, with The Brook Inn at Washbrook a favourite, and it was perfect for me as I could get plenty of exclusive stories for Monday's paper.

When the Blues' team bus arrived at Birmingham City's St Andrew's ground on one occasion, John said to me: 'Let's find a café or pub and have a coffee or something.' This was something he would never normally do. I asked him what this was all about and he said he was going to try a different approach with regard to the build-up at the ground.

'I'm going to leave them alone until just before they go out,' he declared, so John and I went off in search of a coffee. We walked quite a way before finding a corner café.

We ordered two coffees and sat talking to a police constable who was having a break. When it was time for us to leave he offered us a lift back to the ground. I nipped off to the loo and when I came out the policeman and John were having a laugh together. I was soon to find out why.

When John and I got outside, the constable showed us his big transit van. 'I'll get in the front boy, you open the back doors and get in,' said John.

I hopped in without seeing what was ahead. Suddenly I found myself in the company of four police Alsatians.

They all sat motionless, but John warned: 'One word from the constable boy and you might be in trouble.'

I've always been wary of big dogs ever since being bitten by one as a child, so I sat motionless, with the dogs' eyes fixed on me.

When we got to the main entrance at St Andrew's I dashed out of the van with John's words ringing in my ears: 'It's a dog's life, isn't it boy.'

His team played well that day, but they were the ones who got bitten as they lost 1-0.

Sometimes the ref ain't the only whistle-blower

John was a good friend of mine and when the time came to blow the whistle on players who had misbehaved badly, I did what I felt was right.

We were up in Manchester on a Friday night before a game with City at Maine Road and some friends had come over to the hotel to see me. We had a meal and ended up having a late drink in a nightclub just down the road.

To my amazement, and to that of my Manchester pals, we found two Blues players – the England Under-21 pair of Jason Dozzell and Dalian Atkinson – chatting together at the bar. I was wild with anger at what they were doing to their boss, their teammates and their fans and I said to one of my Manchester mates: 'I feel like going up and thumping them.' He told me to stay calm so I took his advice and casually walked up to the pair, two players with whom I had always got on well.

The Ipswich born-and-bred Jason was someone I had always tried to help as much as I could since he made his debut as a 15-year-old schoolboy, while Dalian was a favourite of mine, both as a man and a player.

My opening line was short and sweet. 'You two have made my blood boil. John Duncan is a thoroughly decent man and does not deserve this. Neither do the fans. If you go back to the hotel now, then no more will be said about this. If you don't I'll tell the boss. Believe me, I mean it.'

I gave them 10 minutes, but they stayed put, so I kept my promise and told the manager.

John, who had to make a decision on whether or not to play them, was deeply hurt by what had happened – and so were the pair's teammates.

He played them both and Town lost 4-0.

The following Tuesday afternoon, Jason and Dalian turned up to see me at the office.

'Why did you grass us up,' said Dalian. 'The gaffer has just had us in and fined us loads.'

I told them straight: 'John Duncan is a good and honest man. You two s*** on him from a great height. You deserve all you get and just be thankful that I haven't written about this. Don't push your luck as there's still time to splash you two on the front page.'

I added: 'We've always been mates and I'd like that to stay the same way. I like you both, despite this. You've always been good lads to me before all this.' They left in a huff, but there were handshakes all round a few days later.

However, it was a nasty episode for me and for John.

Hoot if you want a new contract

Midway through his three-year spell as Town manager, I felt that I got John a new contract.

Paul Thompson of the *Sheffield Star* phoned me one morning to say that John was on a list of possible replacements for Howard Wilkinson – who had moved on to Leeds – at Sheffield Wednesday. In actual fact, John was number 10 on the list of the Hillsborough board, but that didn't stop me doing a big 'Owls to swoop for Duncan' story.

There was no contact from the Wednesday folk to the Blues' board, or contact with John himself and in the end

Peter Eustace got the job. But not long after this though, chairman Patrick Cobbold stood up at a shareholders' meeting and spoke of the reported interest in their man. The head of the Blues board duly revealed that John had been given a new contract.

I said to him: 'You owe me. I've got you a new contract.'

He admitted: 'I think you have boy. I'll buy you a drink after the game on Saturday.'

That new deal meant that when he was sacked in May 1990, there was still a year of his contract to go. Soon after his dismissal, I went to his house to see him and said: 'Well, at least you've got a year's money to come.'

He said with a tear in his eye: 'I know Dave, I know, but I really wanted to keep that job.'

I was so sad to see him go and he was gutted.

JOHN DUNCAN

1987-90   Neal Manning

KP too flash – pick the bloke from Chesterfield

WHEN Town appointed John Duncan to succeed Bobby Ferguson, one of the directors, Harold Smith, declared: 'We've just signed the new Bobby Robson.'

Sadly, that did not turn out to be the case. The Duncan era always threatened to get going, but in the end never materialised.

John was not the favourite when they were looking for a new manager. Gillingham boss Keith Peacock and Ian Bowyer, who was in charge at Hereford United at the time, were more fancied, while former Town defender Mick Mills was somebody else they wanted to interview. Mills was then doing well as manager of Stoke City but their chairman, Peter Coates, refused Town permission to speak to him. Town chairman Patrick Cobbold accepted that, saying both he and Coates were gentlemen. They were also close friends.

Peacock interviewed as well as anybody and might have been offered the job, but two directors noticed he had his initials, KP, on the shirt he was wearing and thought that was too flash for Ipswich Town!

Bowyer came up short in the interview and in the end the job was given to Duncan, the former Tottenham striker who was manager of Chesterfield. He had previously been in charge at Hartlepool and Scunthorpe.

Bit boring on the straight and narrow

The first thing John did after taking up the reins at Portman Road was to narrow the pitch – not the greatest omen for the football that was to come over the next three years.

After finishing in the top half of the Second Division table in his first season, there was hope that John could push the team even further on, but his record in the transfer market was not as good as supporters hoped. Players like Glenn Pennyfather, Graham Harbey, David Hill and Neil Woods did not really come up to expectations, but against that striker David Lowe proved an outstanding signing. Central defender David Linighan proved an excellent investment as did the inspirational move to bring back John Wark for a second spell.

Unfortunately, Linighan did not really blossom until John Lyall succeeded John, but that was partly due to the fact that his wife, Kay, lost the baby she was expecting and that naturally knocked the big centre-half off track for some time.

In 1990, the board decided on a change with the vastly-experienced John Lyall moving from West Ham where he had made a big name for himself.

John Duncan then got a job with Radio Suffolk, covering the club he had only recently finished managing, together with co-commentator Bryan Knights. Alas, one of his first jobs was to interview Lyall after a match at Wolverhampton during which the new manager kept calling John 'son'. That proved a bit embarrassing for both parties and it was decided that in future Knights should do the interviews.

John loved living and working in Suffolk, and besides covering Town for the radio station, he also reported on Suffolk's Minor Counties' cricket team.

After his spell at Radio Suffolk, he became a teacher at Hadleigh High School before returning to football management and going back to Chesterfield for the second time. He took the club to the semi-finals of the FA Cup in 1992 against Middlesbrough and only a refereeing decision cost them the chance of going all the way to Wembley. Today, John works for the League Managers' Association.

The Russian invasion heads north

The club made history in 1988 when Sergei Baltacha became the first player from the Soviet Union to play in the Football League. Sergei was, in fact, Ukranian and hated being called a Russian or a 'Ruski'. However, while Town were very much under the spotlight for making this unique signing, it did not really work out as the club had hoped.

David Sheepshanks, then a director, had gone to the Soviet Union on a business trip and had been told that there were plenty of good players that could be signed by English clubs at a cheap price. So John and David flew to the Soviet Union and came back with a specialist sweeper who had been capped 48 times for his country. Strangely, Sergei was played at right-back for Ipswich, a decision he could not understand.

Unable to speak English, the club arranged for an interpreter for Sergei's first season at Portman Road. His name was George Scanlon, who later did a similar job for Andrei Kanchelskis when he went to Manchester United. They also found Sergei a house which was very close to that of our old friend, Bob Shelley. While Sergei

'Wor' Jackie explains the way to the bowling alley.

Bill McGarry.

Neal and Dave with the Festival of Ipswich Challenge Cup (the Evening Star beat Radio Orwell in a match at Chantry Park!)

Neal and Dave again: 'No, you get the coffees!'

Neal at the old Wembley, just a couple of days before the 1978 Cup Final.

The British Press World Ten – Frank McClintock's favourite player front row extreme left.

Jet-setting it in the '70s at Speke Airport. 'Hey Colin, I hear the in-flight entertainment's Bugsy Malone. Well at least we're dressed for it.

'No seriously boys, one day we're going to win the FA Cup!' Bobby leading the laughs with coaches Cyril Lea and Roy McCrohan.

I'm backing
BOBBY
on Nov.13th

Father backs son all the way. Bobby with dad Tom.

Bobby with coaches Cyril Lea, Charlie Woods, Bobby Ferguson and chief scout Ron Gray pose with the FA Cup... and another trophy.

George and Bobby on testimonial night: two legends together.

'Motty, that's my foot son.' Bobby and John Motson play in a charity match at Felixstowe.

The Cobbold brothers celebrate success: 'Quick! Hurry up. It's heavy when it's full.'

Our homecoming heroes parade the Cup at Mick Lambert's testimonial versus a London XI.

Mariner and Gates in training: 'Hey Dave! Hello mate! Here Eric, love those press boys. What a fantastic job it is they do!'

A certain Mr Beattie: 'Kevin son, you were such a star!'

Bobby at home with wife Elsie, son Mark and dogs.

The Hunters at home. Allan with wife Carol and sons Lee and Paul.

Chez Burley. George at home with wife Gill.

Brian Talbot – the domino king!

Bobby Ferguson - the master tactician.

'John 'boy' Duncan shakes on it.

John Lyall with one of his inspired signings Ian Marshall: 'Ponce or parasite, delete as applicable. Never seen that on a contract before boss.'

Joe Royle: 'Oi! Steward! He said something about my dad!'

Jim Magilton: 'Ere, don't they look a bit young Steve?'

Roy Keane at the training ground doing something else he's famous for.

found life difficult in his new surrounding, Bob took him under his wing. He recalls, 'Sergei was always in demand in his first season. He received many invitations and never wanted to let anybody down. He never understood why training finished by lunchtime because it was not something he was used to back home. The drinking culture was another thing he could not get his head around. The only time he ever had a drink was when he had a pint of lager after a game.'

'What a lot of people did not understand was that Sergei was under a lot of pressure. Every month he had to go to London to the Russian Embassy to collect his wages. He was not paid directly by Ipswich Town, but through an agency called Inter Sport. The way Sergei felt that the Russians were controlling him, he thought that his house might be bugged.'

Bob recalled one incident when he was in London with Sergei. He said: 'Sergei had had a call from a journalist who said he worked for Pravda, asking him to meet him at the Royal Kensington Hotel. We were there for about three hours and what I found strange was that the journalist never took a note of anything said. Three weeks later we found out it was in fact someone from the Russian Embassy.'

When John Duncan was sacked and John Lyall took over as manager, Sergei was hoping that he would be offered a new contract. Bob takes up the story. 'Somebody at the club obviously marked John Lyall's card and Sergei was not offered another contract. That left him just five days to find another club before his permit ran out, otherwise he would have to return to the Soviet Union.

'Nobody at Portman Road helped and I was on the phone frantically trying to find him a club. It was former

Town player Ian Redford who came to the rescue. He told me St Johnstone, for whom he was then playing, had been promoted to the Scottish Premier Division and might be interested.

'I spoke to their chairman who said he could offer Sergei a one-year deal, but would give him a further two years if they were not relegated at the end of the season.

'Sergei had been on low wages at Ipswich, but got an improved deal with St Johnstone. The deal was done in time and all over the phone. His whole life changed when he went to play and live in Scotland.

'St Johnstone played him as sweeper and in his first season he was voted player of the year. I missed Sergei after he had moved to Scotland because he had been like a brother to me.'

Sergei was given a further two years' contract and later moved on to play for Inverness Caledonian Thistle, the club which he later managed.

Today he lives in London, but the Baltacha name is kept in the news because of their tennis-playing daughter, Elena, who is one of Great Britain's highest-ranked women players. Their son, Sergei junior, followed in his father's footsteps, starting his football with the Ipswich Junior Blues and going on to play for St Mirren.

JOHN LYALL

1990-94   DAVE ALLARD

A ponce and a parasite!

JOHN LYALL and I had more rows than many married couples, but however severe they were, we always made up.

I liked John, and I know he was quite fond of me. Every time he called me a Suffolk straw sucker, I'd hit back and call him an East End barrow boy.

Some of the rows we had became folklore among media men who were involved with the Town. During one press conference, in front of a good attendance, he threw down his fag packet and lighter to declare: 'I refuse to stay in the room any longer with a ponce and parasite like you.'

He stormed out, but his assistant, Charlie Woods, persuaded him to come back which he duly did, although little more was said by him to me at that conference.

Hello Judy!

There was a time when every time I rang John he would just say 'hello Judy', and then put the phone down. I wondered to myself what this Judy business was all about, so I rang my mate Michael Hart on the *Evening Standard.*

Michael was a good friend of Lyall's and had written his autobiography after he left West Ham following 25 years with the club from player to manager.

'Oh dear,' said Michael. 'You must have upset him badly. We cockney boys say Judy to someone when we mean 'stench'... (Judy Dench).' As it turned out, the 'Judy' bit came about because of an incorrect headline written by a news sub-editor on a front page story of mine, but like many spats in football, it was all soon forgotten and we were back to normal again.

The vastly experienced Blues' chief had taken West Ham to their highest-ever position in the top flight of English football and under his leadership they also won the FA Cup, and what he achieved with Town was immense, taking them into the Premier League and keeping them there for two years.

When I heard John had died suddenly at his Tattingstone home of a sudden heart attack at the age of 66, I was distraught and all sorts of Lyall stories came back into my mind, so here's a choice few.

The smoker's cure

I had turned up at the ground once to see him not long after he'd taken over from John Duncan. Just as I got to the main entrance, he was coming out.

'Ah, just the man. Drive me to Croydons the jewellers me old son,' said John in his broad cockney twang. As we went towards the main gate, John explained: 'I've got to do a little PR job at Croydons, Dave. They want me to open a new part of their jewellery store or something.'

Sadly for manager Len Noye, and the waiting customers, the new Town boss never turned up. I remember vividly turning into a road near the shop when he suddenly barked: 'Stop, stop.' I pulled up immediately. John's knee had locked, the legacy of the cruciate operation that ended his playing career at West Ham when he was only 23. The sweat was rolling off him, he had the passenger side door open and was waggling his leg around to try to release the pain. Two boys walking past recognised him and he even interrupted his waggling to sign autographs.

John then turned to me and said: 'Dave me old son, I'm in agony. Take me back to the ground.'

We went back to Portman Road and he led me to the treatment room.

John sat on the edge of one of the physio's tables with the sweat still pouring off him.

He then said: 'Dave, have you got any fags on you. I've left mine up in the office.'

I gave him a fag and lit it. As he dragged heavily on it, there was a click – the knee had gone into place.

'The old fag calmed me down and did the trick me old son. I should have had it earlier,' said John.

But sometimes I wasn't deemed to be quite so helpful.

Coventry, Finland

I usually went on a summer tour with the Blues' squad, but one close season John banned me from a trip to Finland for something I'd written which had upset him. *The Evening Star* was determined I should go and sent me over independently. I travelled all over the beautiful country by train, but every time I came within sight of John he ignored me.

Steve Sedgley, the new £1 million signing from Tottenham, came up to me on the quiet after one match in the city of Pori and said: 'I've never had any dealings with you, but the lads say you're OK. They think the gaffer has gone over the top in banning you from travelling with us.'

He then added: 'Anything you want to know, ask me.'

Money talks and Allard walks!

It was during the Lyall era that I eventually stopped travelling on the team bus to domestic games. It was my decision and followed a row with his number two, Mick McGiven.

All the media folk were gathered for a pre-match press conference when Mick came in, walked straight up to me and said: 'You're a — —.'

The remark followed a story I had written concerning a rearranged game for Town which was being shown live on Sky and would naturally swell the coffers at Portman Road. However, the match would also cause fixture congestion for the club and senior players such as John Wark and Mick Stockwell were both concerned about the effect it would have on what was essentially a small squad. I used to take Lyall's 'stick' on the chin, but I felt that McGiven's tirade, and my subsequent retaliation, would make life on the bus difficult for both him and me.

Burst bubbles

There was a time when John invited me into the visitors' dressing room at West Ham. It was emotional for him as it was his first visit back after being sacked by the club he joined as a 15-year-old player.

Town had lost 3-1 and I was with a group of journalists waiting for John to appear in the interview area, which was the club foyer.

It was a long wait, as John never came, but suddenly, out of a door came a little bloke in a Hammers' blazer. In a broad cockney accent, he said: 'Dave Allard 'ere?'

My hand went up.

'Follow me son,' he declared.

He took me down the long corridor to the visitors' dressing room.

'There's a geezer in there wants to see you,' was the little steward's next words.

Up in the corner of the dressing room sat John, who said: 'Sit down son. We'll have a chat, but I don't want to go in front of that lot in the foyer. A few of 'em let me down in my final weeks here.'

There was moisture in his eyes as he talked about what it was like to be in the away dressing room at the Boleyn Ground.

'I gave my all for this club for 25 years,' he said.

Then he added: 'Now I'm determined to lift Ipswich up and up.'

He did just that.

The greatest story ever told! (Well, he did look a bit like Jesus)

Even after he retired, John used to wind me up about the time *The Evening Star* carried a story about him being set to sign a world star. 'With the dough we've got available, we couldn't afford one of his boots,' the Blues chief laughed at the time. The player in question was the Argentinian Gabriel Batistuta and at the time he was in Italy with Fiorentina but reported to be unsettled and keen to try his luck in England.

A national newspaper carried two paragraphs saying that Town were interested in him. I found out who had written it and had a chat with him. The reporter admitted it was a total 'flier', as we say in the trade, and there was no substance to it.

However, I was told to follow it up and do a piece for the *Evening Star*. I refused, saying that it was total nonsense. As a result, a colleague was asked to do it and reluctantly did so. I phoned John and told him the story had nothing to do with me. It created a bit of a stir and excited some fans for a little while, but even they soon realised just how ludicrous it was.

For a fortnight afterwards, every time I phoned John and asked if there was anything doing, he would say something like: 'Yes Dave, we're signing Zidane.'

JOHN LYALL

1990-94   Neal Manning

Hammer blow to glory

IT WAS the unanimous decision of the Town board of directors that the club needed an experienced manager to take over from John Duncan. John Lyall, who was out of work after being sacked by West Ham, was the man they targeted.

It was decided that director Ken Brightwell and coach Charlie Woods should go to his Chigwell home to try to persuade him to become Town's new manager. Charlie knew John well, while Ken was thought to be the best person to deal with the financial side.

It certainly wasn't plain sailing trying to lure John to Portman Road. He was still hurt about being sacked by the Hammers, but in the end he agreed to become Town's new boss.

The first thing he did after his appointment was to make the under-achieving David Linighan club captain.

His next target was Jason Dozzell. John told him: 'I was desperate to sign you for West Ham when you were a 15-year-old schoolboy. I had watched you play for Langham Lions in the Colchester Youth League several times, but didn't get you. However, I've got you now.'

There was no doubt, however, that one of John's best signings of all time was Steve Whitton. He proved a key player as Town won the old Division Two Championship and took their place in the inaugural Premier League in 1992.

It was Charlie Woods who played a leading part in bringing Steve to Portman Road. At that time, Steve was floundering in Sheffield Wednesday's reserves, as he undoubtedly had the ability but was not showing it. Charlie persuaded John to take a look at him. He said: 'Charlie took me to Hillsborough to watch a Central League game between Sheffield Wednesday and Preston. I asked him what he thought and Charlie said that he had watched Whitton quite a few times and that we should sign him. So I simply said to him: 'It's up to you, your decision.'

Ron Atkinson, then Wednesday's manager, was sitting across from John and Charlie in the director's box. John told Charlie to go and speak to Atkinson and offer him £100,000.

The offer was accepted and Town never looked back. Steve had had his problems off the field in the past, but he proved a great signing. He was good in the air, quick on the right hand side and instrumental in helping Town win the Second Division Championship. There's no doubt that Town resurrected his career.

Wark on... and on... and on...

John Wark will go down in history as one of the all-time Ipswich Town greats.

The Scot's goalscoring feats from midfield, both at home and abroad, have been well documented, and he proved equally adept as a central defender.

After two spells at Portman Road and spells at both Liverpool and Middlesbrough, Warky did not have a club when the 1991-92 season started.

Still living in Ipswich, he asked John Lyall if he could come and train at Portman Road. John had just signed Eddie Youds from Everton for £200,000, but in his first match at Derby he was caught by Ted McMimm and suffered a bad injury. Frank Yallop was forced to switch from full-back to centre-half because Brian Gayle had been sold to Sheffield United for £800,000. When Wark's name was mentioned as a natural replacement, John Lyall was telling people he thought that his legs had gone and was past his sell-by date. However, he was soon to revise his opinion. After watching him play in a couple of practice matches, he decided to sign him for a third spell at the club until the end of the season.

Wark played his first game at Grimsby and never looked back, going on to win the Player of the Year award. It had turned out to be a tremendous season as Lyall, with considerable help from Charlie Woods, masterminded their success.

The sale of Gayle, for instance, proved instrumental in stabilising the finances of the club. Charlie revealed that Sheffield United had come in with a bid of £350,000, but that was not acceptable and Town wanted £800,000. Dave Bassett, United's manager, knew Gayle well, having brought him through when he was in charge at Wimbledon, so he was prepared to pay the Town asking price. So, with Wark now on board and revelling in a central defensive role, the club had got a player for nothing after banking £800,000 from the sale of Gayle.

Lyall brought the best out of so many players, none more than striker Chris Kiwomya, whom he often called 'my little old boy.'

He also christened Chris 'Lino'. It was the same nickname he had given Trevor Brooking when he was in the youth team at West Ham, the reason being that both players used to spend so much time on their backsides! But John made Chris a much stronger player and they became like a father and son and the banter on the team bus had to be heard to be believed.

Listen up, tractor boy

John Lyall was old school. He was rarely seen on television and like Ron Greenwood, his predecessor at West Ham, went out of his way to keep a low profile. However, he always made sure he looked after the local media, although he found it difficult dealing with regional provincial journalists on a daily basis.

In London, unless there was a big story, he only had to deal with the *Ilford Recorder*.

His achievement in guiding Town to the Second Division Championship in 1992 was phenomenal. At the start of that season they were 25-1 outsiders to win promotion, but his wheeling and dealing with limited resources made it an outstanding feat. Many players regarded him as the best coach with whom they had ever worked. Town midfielder Mick Stockwell reckoned he was different class and that he should have gone on to become the England manager.

John had a special way with each individual and that was testimony to his success as a manager. He was always forthright with directors and never allowed them to ride roughshod over him. A good example was when Steve Whitton was in big trouble again after being convicted of drink-driving for a second time. He was warned that he could face a custodial sentence, but in the end was fined, banned from driving and given community service. That made front page news in the *East Anglian Daily Times* and as a result chairman John Kerr suggested to his manager that he should get rid of Whitton.

John drew on his cigarette and said: 'You're a farmer. You need your fields ploughing urgently, but you've only got one tractor driver. Would you get rid of him? I've only got one Steve Whitton and I can't replace him.'

Point made.

GEORGE BURLEY

December 1994–October 2002   **Dave Allard**

And coming up on the rails!

I HAD a call late one night from a Colchester United player who said: 'The gaffer cleared his desk this afternoon, I'm told. You know what that means.'

It was close to 11pm, but I still rang George Burley, someone I had known since he was a bright eyed 15-year-old apprentice professional at Portman Road. Now he was to be the manager of Ipswich Town. He was coming home, as they say.

I knew he'd been interviewed and had made a big impression, but had walked out on his contract at Layer Road to take the new job.

George picked up the phone at 11.10pm and I said: 'You old so and so. You've come up on the rails like a thoroughbred.'

George replied: 'Aye Dave. What do you think? Sorry I haven't phoned you about it.'

I said: 'George, we've always got on well with you as a player and me a reporter. I'm not sure how we'll get on with our new partnership.'

'Aye, we'll be fine mate,' said George with great assurance.

However, in the early days there were a few problems as I had to write some negative stories, mainly about Town's performances, or rather, lack of them.

George though, was quite gentlemanly about it and said to me: 'I think you're on my back a bit Dave. Give me a break mate.'

I duly did, but his assistant, Dale Roberts, was a bit more forthright.

I was in the club foyer one afternoon when Dale came out from the dressing room area to tell me to 'f— —- off.'

Dale was also a former Town player that I knew well, so I just said: 'Come on Dally old mate. Don't be grumpy because I used to beat you at snooker a few times.'

He soon came round and we laughed about that exchange when I visited him in Ipswich Hospital a few years back just days before cancer claimed his life. When I shook his hand he looked me in the eyes and laughed: 'Keep writing your usual crap.'

George was by Dale's bedside as well and we both cracked up with laughter.

Dale was forthright with me right to the end, but, in truth, we got on well. I respected his work and he respected mine.

Dyer 'nother day!

When David Sheepshanks took over as chairman the stage was set as he announced his five-year plan to put the club back in European competition again. David had the utmost faith in George, even when promotions were not achieved.

Two years after Burley's appointment, following a bad defeat at Charlton, I waited for Sheepshanks in the rain outside the main stand at the Valley.

'We've had a bad defeat and we're having a bad run, but George Burley and I are joined at the hip. We will put this club right together,' said David.

It happened just that way and what proved vital was the arrival on the first-team scene of 17-year-old Kieron Dyer.

A few years later, cash from the £6 million sale of the Ipswich born-and-bred midfielder to Newcastle gave Burley the chance to bring in a succession of bargain buys to achieve promotion – but before all that, there was a time when it was feared Kieron had drowned.

I was on tour with the Blues in Finland and we all went to a small island just off the coast one afternoon for a few beach sports and some swimming.

The tour guide told us not to swim in a certain area as the red warning flag was flying. Kieron heard this, but said to me: 'I'm a terrific swimmer Dave. I'll go out into that dodgy bit.'

Before I could say anything, he'd gone.

I told George and the chairman and the three of us looked out to sea – but we couldn't see a thing.

'Oh my God,' exclaimed the alarmed Sheepshanks. 'What has happened to him?'

Ten minutes went by and we still couldn't see him in the water.

I said to Burley: 'I know his mum and dad, Jackie and Leroy. Surely we aren't going to have to tell them their son has drowned?'

The tour guide was about to phone for the rescue helicopter when suddenly a head popped up from behind a rock.

Kieron came up the beach and said to Burley: 'The water is like a warm bath gaffer.'

Everyone was so relieved to see him that there was no rebuke from anyone, although skipper Matt Holland pulled him to one side back at the hotel for a quiet word. The impish Kieron, a little wizard of a player, crept up to me after our evening meal.

He prodded me in the side and said: 'Did you like my swimming Dave?'

I came back with: 'No, I bloody well didn't. I had fears of writing a "Death on Tour" story.'

He then made me laugh when he said: 'A few bobs' worth of cash would have hit the sea bed had I really gone down, wouldn't it? Just say I kept the gaffer and the chairman on their toes.'

Finidi? George no!

Burley did brilliantly in the English transfer market, but a series of overseas flops contributed to the club diving to relegation and administration. We were on tour in Estonia just after the club had qualified for the UEFA Cup in the first season after promotion. Burley told me he was about to sign a 'world class' player, so I was desperate to find out who it was and send back an exclusive story to the *Evening Star*.

George said he would let me know as soon as he could, but the nature of my job meant I needed to know earlier.

Dutch midfield man Martijn Reuser and I were strolling around the Tallinn hotel when I asked him: 'Do you know who this world class player is?'

'Yes Dave, but I dare not tell you,' he replied.

I pleaded with him, but he remained tight-lipped.

The following morning I found a note had been pushed under my room door. It read: 'Finidi George and this is a terrible mistake. His best days are way gone.'

Tens of thousands of Town voices would later echo that comment.

GEORGE BURLEY

December 1994–October 2002   Neal Manning

You won't be needing those trainers Howard

JOHN LYALL had once said that the day he didn't enjoy getting on the team bus, he would pack it in. That day came in November 1994 after just over four years at the helm and at a time when Town were going through a rough patch. So the search for a successor began, with Mick McGiven holding the reins until the appointment of George Burley a month later.

The choice of a new manager, however, appeared to be between Graham Turner, then the football director at Hereford United, and former Everton player and manager, Howard Kendall. Turner was interviewed by the board in Cambridge and while he knew Kendall was also in the frame, he said he had a feeling there was someone in the background that could come through on the rails.

Kendall travelled down from Liverpool by train one Tuesday for his interview. He was picked up at Ipswich Station by secretary David Rose and taken straight to the Talbooth Hotel in Dedham, on the Suffolk-Essex border, to meet the full board of directors. He was obviously very confident of landing the job because he brought his football boots with him so that he could take training the next day!

After the interviews, Town chairman John Kerr told his fellow directors that he would like them to interview one more candidate. Director Ken Brightwell later admitted that they did not know that Burley was in the frame. The Scot, who had also been a former Town full-back, was currently the manager of Colchester United.

But Brightwell said: 'George swept us off our feet with the ideas he had for our club. His interview was nothing short of sensational. We all agreed that he was the man for us.'

Coincidentally both Kerr and Burley hailed from Ayrshire, but this did not have the slightest bearing on him landing the job. The Town chairman said it was the right time for Burley to be the manager of Ipswich Town, although Colchester, understandably, were not too happy at their neighbours poaching their man.

And Graham Turner was proved to be right about a dark horse being in the frame.

...and for those of you who may have forgotten...

Not long after George had taken over as the new manager, Town suffered a disastrous 9-0 defeat at the hands of Manchester United in which Andy Cole scored five goals.

George admitted that it was the lowest point of his career and the scoreline would have been even bigger but for goalkeeper Craig Forrest who made a number of great saves.

At that time Town's form was poor, and Tony Garnett, who was covering the game for the *East Anglian Daily Times* that day, went into the press room before the game waving betting slips for a 5-0, 6-0 and 7-0 victory for United.

Jimmy Armfield, the former Blackpool and England defender, who was working for *BBC* radio, and ex-United legend Paddy Crerand, also on media duties, were both highly amused by Tony's bets. They both thought, however, he was way off the mark.

When United's fifth goal went in all heads turned towards Tony and even more so when the score became six and then seven. Even Tony could not have visualised that the final scoreline would end one short of double figures.

Having put that defeat behind him, George concentrated on improving the squad and made some astute signings including Jamie Clapham from Tottenham and Jermaine Wright from Crewe, while later on he added David Johnson from Bury and Marcus Stewart from Huddersfield Town.

Shame! There's only one Kevin Phillips

In 1995 David Sheepshanks took over as chairman from John Kerr, declaring that he had a five-year plan to have the club in the Premiership as well as challenging for Europe within that time. He achieved it when Town returned to the big time after beating Barnsley in the 2000 Play-off Final at Wembley. That aim, however, might have been achieved earlier had it not been for the negativity of the board.

George wanted to sign Kevin Phillips, a 24-year-old striker from Watford for £350,000. Although he had been injured for much of the previous season, Phillips turned up at Portman Road to have a medical and sign a three-year contract. He lived in Royston, Hertfordshire, and playing for Town would have been the ideal move for him, but at the very last moment Sheepshanks pulled the plug on the deal. His reasoning was that the club could not take the risk of forking out £350,000 because they did not know what fee an FA tribunal would set for defender Tony Vaughan's transfer to Manchester City.

The board were stunned when the tribunal told City that they would have to pay £1.3 million. Had Ipswich known that earlier, it's safe to say the Phillips deal would have gone through.

Phillips was disappointed, especially as he could have continued to live at Royston and play for Town, but their loss was Sunderland's gain. Peter Reid, then in charge at Roker Park, quickly stepped in.

Phillips soon struck up a partnership with Niall Quinn and they became a goalscoring sensation in the north-east. George had no doubts that if he had been able to sign Phillips, a partnership with James Scowcroft would have taken the club in to the Premiership earlier than 2000, when they beat Barnsley 4-2 in the Play-off Final at Wembley.

JOE ROYLE

November 2002–May 2006   Dave Allard

Nearly broke the Hasselbaink

JOE ROYLE once told me that he had a plan up his sleeve to bring Dutch strike ace Jimmy Floyd Hasselbaink to Portman Road. We were having a bit of lunch in the Rushmere Falcon, just down from the training ground. Town were not far off the top of the Championship and had high hopes of gaining automatic promotion. The March transfer deadline was looming with the campaign on the verge of the run-in.

Joe leaned across the table and said to me: 'Keep this to yourself pal, but I'm having a go at getting Jimmy Floyd Hasselbaink down here.'

What a shock. I was flabbergasted. I did keep it to myself at the time, but I have no qualms talking about it now.

Joe went on: 'Jimmy can set the place alight and get us up.'

At the time, Hasselbaink was down the pecking order at Jose Mourinho's Chelsea.

Alas, the Right-Royle plan back-fired when an injury crisis at Stamford Bridge saw Hasselbaink back on the bench for a match at Bolton. He duly came on, scored a hat-trick, and stayed firmly on the first team scene in the Premier League.

'Oh well, it was worth a try. It could have come off. There was no harm in having a go,' said Joe.

When Ipswich lost to West Ham in the play-offs, Joe said: 'Jimmy would have landed us the title, I'm sure of that.'

Joe senior

Joe used to love telling me stories about his father, Joe senior.

'The old man was a musician and a good one,' he once said. 'He never got much further than the Merseyside pub and club scene, but so many people said he should have gone to London and bigger things.'

The Royle family lived in a council house in the Liverpool district of Norris Green and Joe was an only child.

'Dad was my hero and when I first got into the Everton team at 16, people said: "That's Joe Royle's son",' he added. 'Dad was so well known around Liverpool. He was the number one Joe Royle.'

Joe junior once saw the late Joe senior as an extra in an old black and white film.

'He was playing in a band and it brought tears to my eyes,' said the Blues chief.

Smoke, smoke everywhere and not a ball to kick

Another thing that used to bring tears to Joe's eyes was cigarette smoke – as he loathed smoking.

Former Town boss John Lyall was a 40-a-day man and Joe once said to me about him: 'He was a nice chap and we did a few deals between us, but I always found it hard to get close to him though. I mean getting close in a physical sense. If you got within half a yard of John he was blowing smoke in your face.'

Joe once admitted that, oddly enough, smoking helped to make him a professional player.

He explained: 'We lived in a small house. Dad smoked, mum smoked and granddad smoked, so I used to have to run to the park and get some fresh air. Usually when I got there I found a game of football going on.'

When he got into the Everton first team at 16, he found that so many of the players smoked.

The skipper was a Welsh international midfielder named Roy Vernon and he was a chain smoker and Joe said: 'It would never have surprised me had he led the team out smoking a fag! Believe it or not, I once saw him standing in the showers at Goodison Park with a fag in his mouth. Somehow he managed to shower and at the same time keep his cigarette dry and burning!'

You'll win nothing with kids

Joe did a grand job on a shoestring at Portman Road. He lifted the team immediately, and they rose up the table to just miss out on the play-offs.

The following season they were within a hair's breadth of automatic promotion and then they lost to West Ham in the play-off semi-finals.

His third season was mediocre, but he kept the Blues' heads above water.

Winning the FA Youth Cup during his time in charge possibly worked against him, he once confided to me. He said: 'It's great for the young players of course and wonderful prestige for the club, the Academy staff especially, but it can bring problems for a manager, because directors get the idea that a top youth team will automatically develop into the bulk of a good first team. Some of our board felt that there was no need to go into the transfer market too much and had a "kids can do it" attitude.'

Joe went on: 'A successful youth team doesn't guarantee a big influx into the first team, but putting that across to directors can bring problems.'

Backing up what Joe said, I recall John Lyall once saying: 'I'd rather have a youth team bottom of the League, but one which produces one top player, than a youth team winning everything, but just sending forth a batch of average players not really good enough for the level at which your senior side is playing.'

Brief encounter

At the end of his last season as Town boss, Royle told the Town board that, after that term's mediocre finish, realistically, it would be similar the following campaign due to the lack of funds. They initially accepted this somewhat downbeat appraisal and he went back to his Ormskirk home for a break. However, some members of the board did not like what they had heard and another meeting was called. This would be for directors only and it was decided that it would be for the best if Joe went.

Chairman David Sheepshanks travelled north to Crewe where he met Royle at the train station and told him there was a general consensus among the board that a new face was needed at the helm of the club.

'It was an amicable meeting, but we were both upset. David and I shook hands at the end with tears in our eyes,' said Joe.

JOE ROYLE

November 2002–May 2006   **Neal Manning**

Smokin' Joe will be a knockout

THERE was no doubt in Paul Hince's mind that Town had landed the perfect manager when Joe Royle was appointed in November 2002. Paul, a former Manchester City winger who was understudy to the legendary Mike Summerbee, and also played for Charlton, Bury and Stockport, had worked closely with Joe for years in his duties of reporting on Oldham Athletic for the *Manchester Evening News*. So when Joe came to Suffolk, Paul gave this ringing endorsement. 'You won't find a better CV anywhere in football. He's a great manager and has a great coach working with him in Willie Donachie. You'll find him a delight to deal with.'

Paul himself was a real character and recalled the day he was playing for Bury when there was a break in play because of a serious injury. He simply wandered over to the touchline where he smoked a cigarette that he had cadged from a fan! Joe used to call Paul 'The Weasel', while Paul nicknamed him 'Smoking Joe' after he had been banned from smoking on the Oldham team bus.

When Joe was appointed Town manager he had already taken Manchester City from the First Division to the Premiership, while at Everton in his first season they had won the FA Cup and at unfashionable Oldham he had taken them to the FA Cup semi-finals and into the Premiership.

Tenner for a new keeper? Anybody?

Humour always played a big part in everything he did whether it was in the dressing room, with the staff or the press. To emphasise how precarious the financial situation was at Portman Road, when asked who he was going to sign, he said: 'I'm not going to spend my own money!'

After one match when describing goalkeeper Kelvin Davis' attempt to make a save, he joked: 'He went down in instalments!'

Although he did not take over until November, Town almost made the top six, and when they did the following year they were beaten by West Ham in the play-offs.

Chair we go!

Joe could always laugh at himself and I was told that there was only one occasion when he really lost his cool badly. Ian Marshall, a former Town player, had riled him so much when they were at Oldham that Joe picked up a chair from the corner of the dressing room and declared later: 'I think I would have smashed it over Marshy's head.' Fortunately, his assistant, Willie Donachie, stepped in at the vital moment and grabbed the chair, otherwise Joe might have found himself appearing at Oldham Magistrates' Court.

(Not quite) Murder in Long Melford

When he arrived at Ipswich, the local pressmen didn't know what he was going to be like to deal with because they had heard of a problem that he'd had at Everton.

Joe felt that there had been a vendetta against him and it got to a stage when some things written about him on Merseyside – even though he was a Scouser – upset his mother and father. One reporter, in particular, got Joe's back up big time, and Joe just couldn't understand the flak he was taking, as Everton had won the FA Cup and were near the top of the League with no money to spend. Joe decided to quit, much to the disappointment of chairman Bill Kenwright.

At Portman Road, Joe proved to be a miracle worker in the way he revitalised the club. A very sensitive man, he would read everything written about the club in the local papers. There was a time when a man from Long Melford used to continually write to one newspaper criticising Joe, and he thought about going to visit him, presumably to give him a piece of his mind, until he was advised that wouldn't be a good idea.

One of Joe's great qualities was that he made everybody feel important and one of the security men at Portman Road said after he had left the club that he would always stop to talk come rain or shine. In his opinion there would never be another Joe Royle at the club.

Sky-dive to bread Line

He was always full of stories of his time at Oldham and of his great relationship with chairman and long-serving FA member Ian Stott. Ian was always trying to save a bit here and a bit there and Joe recalled the time when he was about to offer £40,000 for a player. The chairman told him to offer £35,000, but Joe was convinced that would not be accepted. As it turned out it was, and it led to the remarkable sight of one of football's longest-serving chairmen dancing with delight around the boardroom table, shouting: 'I told you they would take £35,000.'

Joe had proved a dab hand in the transfer market as was amply illustrated when he signed Shefki Kuqi from Sheffield Wednesday for a small fee for Town. He turned out to be joint leading goalscorer with Darren Bent with 20 goals apiece in the 2004-05 season and a year later Premiership club Blackburn Rovers paid £1 million for him.

But Joe used to worry himself sick about Shefki's sky-dive celebrations after he had scored a goal because he thought one day he would injure himself.

Joe once told him: 'If you ever break anything doing that stupid dive, I'll fine you a year's wages.'

He was also a master at improving players, both young and old. One young player who particularly blossomed was Owen Garvan, the Irishman who was in the Academy when Joe took over. Joe gave him so much confidence that at one stage he claimed Owen could become the next Steven Gerrard if they looked after him properly. That might have been a bit of a tall order, but I always felt that a continuation of Joe and Willie Donachie's work could have seen him be a much better player than he is today.

Whiff of Carrow? Surely not!

JOE was often amazed at the naivety of the directors at Portman Road, but they were no different to any others in thinking you could wave a magic wand.

He used to say: 'I'm a window shopper and can rarely afford to buy.' Joe got on well with the majority of the board at Portman Road, but always felt that one of them, Kevin Beeston, didn't like him. Sometimes Joe found his questioning of him at board meetings puzzling. Now and again he felt like blowing his top, but instead bit his tongue.

Joe also felt that Town fans never really took to him. 'I sometimes got the feeling many of them resented the fact that I once played for Norwich, but perhaps it was just me.'

JIM MAGILTON

June 2006–April 2009   Dave Allard

Now, light the blue touch paper...

WHEN Jim Magilton was an Ipswich player, I got on with him like a house on fire – for the vast majority of the time.

There was, however, the odd hiccup, or should I say, the occasional massive cough, and while still a Town player, Jim once gave a very big clue about how he would be as a manager.

It happened when he was playing for Northern Ireland and was substituted after a very short amount of time. Officials said the early departure from the field at Windsor Park in Belfast, was due to injury, but I found out a completely different reason.

I discovered that Jim was substituted so that he could fly back to England and be at the bedside of his sick son, Adam, in Ipswich. Adam had an illness that had dogged him all his life and he was having a desperately bad night, but on this occasion, with dad by his side, he pulled through.

The following morning I phoned Jim and told him I knew the reason for the rush back to Suffolk. He put a bit of meat on the bone, but insisted: 'Keep it low key if you can Dave.'

I made no reply, as I knew that wasn't possible. It was a front page splash if ever there was one and that night the story was on the front page of the *Evening Star*.

...and stand well back!

A few days later I was coming out of the training ground's main entrance when Jim pulled up in his car and flew at me. 'I should throw you over that f——ing hedge, you bastard,' he roared.

'By splashing that stuff about my son you will hold a poor little schoolboy up to ridicule. My lad will take stick in the school playground because of what you've done,' he continued.

I invited him to try and throw me over the hedge, but just as I think he was about to, Blues' assistant manager Dale Roberts came out and restored order.

Not long afterwards, Jim and I made up and we resumed our usual good relationship, but a nerve had certainly been touched and I was to see that side of him again when he became the Town's manager.

Unemployed magician seeks new wand

While he was still a Town player, I used to ghost-write his 'Gentleman Jim' column in the *Evening Star.* Jim was full of amusing stories and good comments and each week I looked forward to doing the feature.

The midfield pass-master was also a very useful contact in general and on one occasion he phoned me to tip me off that the club were poised to sign Jermaine Wright from Crewe for £400,000.

Towards the end of his last season as a player, Jim was out of the side as boss Joe Royle experimented a bit with younger players. The popular player, nicknamed 'Magic' by the fans, came and spent time with me in the press room before the last match of the season.

As he tucked into his chicken and ham pie and sipped his coffee, I said: 'What's happening Jim boy. Where's the next move for you?'

He paused before replying: 'You tell me Dave. You tell me.'

I said: 'Well, if Joe goes, then steam in and apply for the manager's job.'

He felt it might be too early for him but I urged him to go for it if the opportunity arose. However, the way it worked out, I wish I'd kept my mouth shut.

Not long after the season ended, Royle had gone and Jim phoned me at home. 'I'm taking your advice and going in for the job,' he said, before asking me to advise him on what to put in his letter of application to chairman David Sheepshanks.

Joe had told the board the truth by saying that with the resources at hand, Championship mediocrity would probably continue, but that honest assessment had cost him his job.

I rang Joe and asked him what his former skipper should say. He didn't hold back and said Jim should tell the board a different tale to the one he had and paint a brighter picture.

I relayed his thoughts to Jim and he took Joe's advice and duly got the job, to the dismay of Nigel Pearson who came a close second.

Pearson, now manager of Leicester, later told me: 'My wife has family in East Anglia. Ipswich is a great club and it would have been perfect for me, but it wasn't to be.'

So into the Portman Road hot seat Jim went with the experienced coaching pair of Steve Foley and Bryan Klug working with him.

On the way up... on the way down

In his early days in charge I spent quite a bit of time on the phone with Jim and it intrigued me that he seemed to be almost paranoid about how stories were getting out of the club and into the local and national press.

Jim kept asking me to reveal who the 'moles' were and I used to say: 'Look Jim, I'll tell you when you're older. That will probably be when you start taking the old age pension.'

He wasn't happy and on one occasion concluded a call with the words: 'You help me and I'll help you.'

I had the last word by declaring: 'Look Jim, I've already helped you to get this job.'

From there onwards, our relationship did not go very well. Jim spoke to me at press conferences, but there was little personal contact any more.

The experienced Joe Royle had been a delight to deal with, through good times and bad, but now I was dealing with a new boy to the job who, it appeared, was going to ride rough-shod over certain press folk.

I rang him one day on his mobile and he said: 'Look, I'm working. Don't interrupt me when I'm working.'

I sent him an e-mail that read: 'I'm working too Jim.' I then added: 'It has been said that the more the monkey goes up the tree, the more you see of his backside. There's another saying I like too. You meet the same people on the way down as you do on the way up.'

Don't get me wrong, I genuinely liked Jim in so many ways and I got on exceptionally well also with his wife Collette and really hoped he would succeed as Town boss.

Red mist to China

During his playing days, Jim once told me: 'When the red mist comes down I'm a different bloke.' In my view, it came down too often to bring success.

Ex-England coach John Gorman was brought in as an assistant manager to be a calming influence. Press conferences had made Jim so edgy that John was sent in to face the media and John once told me: 'Look Dave, you know that Jim's a good lad really, but he's young and new to this side of the game. He's gone at it a bit "bull in a china shop" and it's rebounded on him.'

JIM MAGILTON

June 2006–April 2009   Neal Manning

Working magician in need of assistant

WHETHER or not it made any difference in the long run, Jim Magilton did not have an assistant manager for some while after his appointment.

After appointing Steve Foley and Bryan Klug as first team coaches, Jim was looking to bring in Terry Cooper, the former England and Leeds United full-back, who had coached him when he was at Southampton for three seasons between 1994-97.

Jim had been Saints' manager Alan Ball's second signing for £600,000 from Liverpool and had been impressed by Terry's coaching abilities at The Dell.

Terry then turned to management, and when Jim wanted him to come to Portman Road, the timing was not right. Terry had managed Bristol Rovers and Exeter City, but after leaving the Devon club, he suffered an illness. As a result, he decided against taking up Jim's offer because of health issues. It was a big disappointment to Jim who felt that his experience would have made him an ideal right- hand man.

Terry's son Mark, who has managed Northampton, Peterborough, Kettering and Darlington, said his father was very tempted by Jim's offer, but unfortunately had to let him down and it was not until December 2008 that Jim finally got an assistant with John Gorman agreeing to become his number two. The pair later linked up at QPR, while Gorman, who played for Celtic, Carlisle and Tottenham as a player, also worked with Glen Hoddle when he was England manager.

Lovable poacher turned gamekeeper

To a certain extent, Jim was a poacher turned gamekeeper. When Bryan Hamilton, the former Town winger, was manager of Northern Ireland, he said his three most difficult players to handle were Gerry Taggart, Iain Dowie and Magilton.

There was once an incident on a plane that resulted in Hamilton leaving all three out of Northern Ireland's next two internationals.

Going from player to manager at Portman Road saw him change his personality. He went from lovable old Jim as a player to a fiery individual as a manager.

Press conferences became very tetchy affairs, and people didn't understand why he had it in for the media. It came to a head at one Portman Road Press conference when he started having a go at Derek Davis, the then correspondent of the *East Anglian Daily Times.*

It turned into a nasty scene. Fellow journalists started sticking up for Davis, so Jim decided to get up and walk out. Dave Allard tried to calm Jim down, and all he got for his efforts was: 'Don't tell me what to f***ing do.'

After that, the chickens came home to roost as far Jim was concerned. Davis had his tape recorder going throughout that Press conference and everything that was said had been recorded. The *EADT* and *Evening Star* decided to print the transcript word for word.

That didn't go down well with the club's board of directors, but they decided that John Gorman would take the Press conferences in the future.

Steve Foley kept morale up in the dressing room and on the training ground in his jokey style, but so many people wondered why Jim had turned. He was suspicious of everybody, a far cry from his days at Liverpool where he cleaned John Wark's boots.

Easy on the old boy – especially you Trotter!

On the training ground, manager Jim liked to play in practice matches, but occasionally took exception to players who went in hard on him.

Foley and Klug used to have to put an arm round him to try to calm him down or suggest he should stop playing in training games. A few players saw these type of matches as an ideal way of letting off steam at their manager.

Jim wasn't getting any younger and the fact he couldn't compete in the way he would have liked added to his frustrations.

He also seemed to have it in for certain players and one of his targets was Liam Trotter, the young Ipswich born-and-bred midfield player who is now a key man at Millwall. Stories filtered out to newspapermen, via Trotter's mother, who claimed that Jim treated her son too severely.

In hindsight, the Ipswich directors could have been forgiven for making a mistake in appointing Jim Magilton as manager.

ROY KEANE

April 2009-January 2011   Dave Allard

Now, light the royal blue touchpaper...

THE Roy Keane era with Town was a bit of a white-knuckle ride for hacks like me and there were some white-hot situations when I feared that firebrand-player-turned-firebrand-boss might completely explode.

They always say that you should never be intimidated by anyone, so at press conferences, I always made a point of going up to the podium to shake his hand and look him straight in the eyes before we started.

The former Manchester United icon always obliged in that respect, but one major bust-up stopped the little pre-conference ritual of mine. Or at least, Roy stopped it when he did not offer his hand as usual.

It all stemmed from a sound-off that Keane and I had one Thursday afternoon in the Portman Road media suite at one of his meetings. Attendances at his talk-ins were always high and sometimes there were reporters from his native Republic of Ireland and his home city of Cork in particular, such was the newsworthy attraction of the man.

On this particular afternoon I asked him why he had felt it necessary to say that critical fans 'knew nothing about the game'. One thing led to another and he began to sound like a stuck record as he kept on repeating: 'You're talking bloody nonsense, you're talking bloody nonsense.'

He seemed to be sulking a little about the fan criticism, so I said to him: 'You're treated like royalty at this club and in the region in general.'

...and stand ...well, a bit closer actually

Oh boy, did I touch a raw nerve with that comment. 'What do you mean?' he demanded to know, so I replied calmly: 'The players treat you like royalty, the staff at the club treat you like royalty and everyone in general seems to treat you like royalty. I've never known a manager to be treated as regally as you Roy.'

A club press officer intervened and said: 'OK, Dave, that's enough,' but I was not to be denied and continued: 'What's more, the majority of the media treat you like royalty too. You're treated like royalty and you know it.'

The Town manager then looked away mouthing: 'Rubbish, rubbish. It's all bloody rubbish.'

Tom Williams, the *BBC Look East* sports presenter, said to me when the conference was over: 'Your little spat with Roy was the best cabaret I've seen for ages.' I replied: 'Perhaps he'll blank me now after that, but I reckon he will be a man about it.'

Sure enough he was and took questions from me at the next meeting and was particularly revealing with his answers.

Look Roy, If I don't write it...

Another spat we had came after I wrote a story revealing that his coach Gary Ablett had terminal cancer.

I had been tipped off that the former Liverpool and Everton defender had been taken seriously ill at the Town's Playford Road training ground and had returned to his Merseyside home. Following a pre-season friendly with West Ham, I approached club doctor Steve Roberts to confirm my tip-off and although his facial expression said it all he just said: 'You know I can't discuss someone's medical information.'

I then went to find Keane, who was holding his press briefing near the tunnel as it had been decided not to drag the manager up to the media suite after a pre-season game like this.

After he had finished with a group of reporters, I said to him: 'Can I have a private word?' We moved away from the pack and I told him I knew about Gary's condition. Roy said: 'He felt ill at the training ground and has gone home. Just leave it at that.'

However, if I hadn't written the story, another journalist would, given the information I'd been given. At the next conference, Keane beckoned me towards the podium and blurted out: 'You've let me down badly.' I asked him what he meant and he replied: 'Gary Ablett. That's what I'm on about.'

'Kevin son, you were such a star!' Take two

Roy rarely signed autographs, but he once signed one for me when manager of Sunderland. He had brought his Blacks Cats to Ipswich for a Championship match and just before he came into the media suite, Kevin Beattie asked me if I'd get the match programme signed by him for a friend of his who was a big Manchester United fan.

Graham Anderson of the *Sunderland Echo* told me that he would probably shun me, but I gave it a go for Kevin, the iconic former Town and England defender, then working for local radio.

When Roy came off the podium I confronted him and said: 'Would you sign this programme for Kevin Beattie please.' Roy said: 'Kevin Beattie? **THE** Kevin Beattie?' I said: 'Yes, **THE** Kevin Beattie.'

I pointed out to Roy where Kevin was sitting and he immediately signed the programme and waved to him, before saying: 'He was a fantastic player.'

I went back to my press pals at the bar feeling rather proud of myself, but I wondered if he would have signed had I not said it was for Kevin Beattie. 'I doubt it,' said Wearside scribe Anderson – and he was probably right.

The men with no names on Songs of Praise

During his spell at Ipswich, I never heard Roy call a journalist by their first name. In fact, he made a point of not doing it. He knew most of the names all right, but he never gave any of us the courtesy of using them and it seemed clear to all of us that he had little respect for the media in general.

Despite that, he usually gave us good value for money and newspaper folk, together with our colleagues from television and radio, used to draw him on all sorts of subjects. On one occasion, he was asked about the subject of his faith by Tom Williams of the BBC and in the end, Roy said: 'Look, I'm an Irish Catholic. I take Mass, my wife takes Mass, my kids take Mass. What else do you want to know.'

At this point Terry Baxter, the then communications director, interjected and said: 'Hey Tom, what is this, Songs of Praise?' The conversation ended there and we got back to talking about football, but the reason the question had been asked was that Roy had initially said something like 'I pray we get the right result'.

...And get over the hand of God!

Roy's tirade from the Portman Road media suite podium after a disputed goal by France's Thierry Henry sent the Republic of Ireland out of the World Cup, had to be heard to be believed.

The whingeing by his fellow countrymen had the Town boss repeating: 'Get over it, get over it,' and he then turned his sharp tongue in the direction of those who run the game in the Republic, but much of it was a throwback to what happened when he walked out on manager Mick McCarthy and the squad at the 2002 World Cup Finals in South Korea and Japan.

During his time at Portman Road, his words filled page after page in newspapers and took up a lot of TV and radio time. The Blues had certainly appointed a high profile boss, but although he gave good value with his words, he didn't do the same in terms of Championship points.

I crossed swords with him more than anyone, but Roy never frightened me as I stood up to him.

As a result of that, his aides told me he respected me for it and although he was a real challenge and could be a reporter's nightmare, in a funny sort of way I liked him.

ROY KEANE

April 2009–January 2011   Neal Manning

Fishy business from Mr X

NOW were we to compare Jackie Milburn, the manager with whom we began, with the one with whom we end, Roy Keane, you couldn't have two more opposite personalities, but when it came to Ipswich Town they did have a couple of things in common. Just like Jackie, Roy was a legend as a player, but his reign as manager at Portman Road, which also lasted under two years, was hardly a roaring success. The Irishman had his good points, but to say he could come across a bit aloof and even strange was an understatement.

One way in which this came across to both public and football people was his attitude to signing autographs, and obviously when you're Roy Keane you tend to get asked a lot. In his early days as Town boss, he rented a house at Aldeburgh and on one occasion went to the fish and chip shop near his home to order a meal for his family. The owner spotted his famous customer and made a right fuss of him, giving him extra fish and chips as well as cans of Coca-Cola. After the owner's female assistant had wrapped up the food, she asked him for his autograph, but he refused to sign, saying it was his day off!

Later, he moved to Woodbridge where he was often seen walking his dogs and one day he stopped near some tennis courts to watch a couple of lads who were playing. He said well done to the boys, but when they asked him for his autograph they too got the cold shoulder.

The same thing happened after a League Cup tie at Shrewsbury, when a couple of journalists asked him for his autograph following the post-match press conference, but again he turned them down.

Roy is not alone in this respect as the great golfer Tiger Woods wouldn't sign autographs in his early days on instructions of his management team. They believed that by doing so his signature would be devalued, but, when it comes to such innocent and friendly exchanges in quiet Suffolk villages, it all sounds a bit strange to me.

Drive the f***ing bus ...and I'll buy you a pint

During his time as Town manager, Roy was a complex individual who often spoke without thinking about the effect his words or manner would have on others. On one occasion, Town were travelling to Stansted Airport and this time there was a different driver for the coach journey from Portman Road.

Roy sat on the front seat and put his legs over the rail in front of him. The driver politely asked him not to do it as it could get him into trouble with health and safety issues. Roy simply barked: 'Drive the f***ing bus.' He was determined to make his point and it was not until some 30 miles later that he moved his legs. However, when the coach arrived at its destination, he slipped the driver some money for a drink!

Roy could be extremely kind and considerate and this is a classic example which took the recipient by surprise. The dressing room area steward's wife had died around Christmas time a few years earlier and he was particularly low at this time of year. Someone told Roy of the steward's predicament and that he was down in the dumps, so he slipped him a £50 note and said to have a drink on him.

But tell them f***ing lies, and you can buy your own

One of Roy's most spectacular tirades was at Peterborough following a League Cup defeat and this time his target was Derek Davis, then the *East Anglian Daily Times* football correspondent. Various views had been exchanged between the two of them about a story Derek had written alleging three players would not play for the club again. It all became very heated and ended with Terry Baxter, then the club's communications director, ushering Keane out of the press conference at London Road. As was his way, Keane was determined to have the last word. He shouted at Derek: 'F***ing lies, f***ing lies, f***ing lies.'

Paul – no pal of mine

Living in Aldeburgh and Woodbridge provided the perfect havens for Roy to detach himself from football. Aldeburgh is regarded as one of the most upmarket and possibly snobbish towns in the country with little interest in football. It was a perfect place for him to live as was Woodbridge, another wealthy Suffolk town.

The inhabitants of Aldeburgh and Woodbridge were not interested in discussing football or asking Roy for his autograph and he enjoyed the solitude of walking his dogs. He became quite popular as a dog walker along the promenade at Aldeburgh and around the quayside at Woodbridge and one woman said Roy used to make a fuss of her dog.

Roy once said that dogs were the most loyal creatures he had ever dealt with and added: 'I don't trust anybody, sometimes not even my wife and family. But I trust my dogs.' He was forever stressing his early life wasn't particularly easy, and was told he was too small to become a professional footballer.

'At the ages of 14 and 15 I played in a senior league with big men. It was a tough grounding, but stood me in good stead. I came from the toughest council estate in Cork.'

At press conferences at Portman Road, which were often attended by Irish journalists, Roy was often in his element talking and giving his opinions on almost any given subject. When asked to say a few words about Manchester United midfielder Paul Scholes, his tribute was gushing. He praised him in every way possible. Then somebody asked if Scholes was a friend of his, and Roy simply said 'no!'

And on that note...

Well, thank you very much ladies and gentlemen, we hope you've enjoyed our rollercoaster reminiscences. We started off the way we began, with a footballing giant, one a gentle Geordie, the other neither gentle nor from the Tyneside area, and both of whom, it would be fair to say, found the world of football management a bit hot to handle. Between their brief reigns we hope you'll agree we've bought you a different kind of insight into a range of personalities, loyal servants all who were all united in one thing, wanting the best for a great club. But our final word has to go to the footballing giant who may have had a most distinguished playing career, but unlike the men mentioned above, found true football greatness on the managerial stage. And just like 'Wor Jackie' will be forever Newcastle United's so Our Bobby will always be Ipswich Town's, despite the great job he did in his native Tyneside towards the end of his career.

This book is dedicated to his memory.